Claudio Magris

VOICES: THREE PLAYS

To Have Been, Stadelmann, Voices

TRANSLATED FROM THE ITALIAN
BY PAUL VANGELISTI

GREEN INTEGER
KØBENHAVN & LOS ANGELES
2007

GREEN INTEGER BOOKS
Edited by Per Bregne
København / Los Angeles

Distributed in the United States
by Consortium / Perseus Distribution
Distributed in Europe by Turnaround Publisher Services,
Unit 3, Olympia Trading Estate, Coburg Road, Wood Green,
London N22 6TZ, Phone 44 (0)20 88293009

Green Integer
6022 Wilshire Boulevard, Suite 200A
Los Angeles, California 90036 USA
(323) 857-1115 · *www.greeninteger.com*

First Green Integer Edition 2007
English language copyright © 2007 by Paul Vangelisti
"Stadelmann" was first published in Italy as *Stadelmann*
(Milano: Garzanti Editore, 1988); "Voices" first
appeared in *Le Voci* (Milano: Garzanti Editore, 1995)
Copyright © 1988, 1995, by Claudio Magris
This book is published through agreement between
the Istituto Italiano di Cultura and Claudio Magris.
Back cover copy © 2007 by Green Integer

Design: Per Bregne
Typography: Concord Editorial and Design
Cover photograph: Claudio Magris

LIBRARY OF CONGRESS CATALOGING IN PUBLICATION DATA

Claudio Magris
Voices: Three Plays
ISBN 978-1-933382-81-4
p. cm – Green Integer 187
I. Title II. Series III. Translator

Green Integer books are published for Douglas Messerli

Contents

Claudio Magris

TO HAVE BEEN

To Luca Doninelli

To Have Been

And so Jerry is dead, never mind, that isn't the problem, neither for him nor anyone else, not even for me who loved him and still love him, because love doesn't conjugate—my God, in that sense, of course, what's next, though love has its grammar and doesn't know tenses only verbal moods, in fact, just one, the present infinitive, when you love it's forever and the rest doesn't matter. Any love, any kind of love. It's not true that you get over it, nothing goes away, and this is often the particular rub, but you carry it along with you, like life, and even that is not really such great luck, except that you get over love even less than life. It's there, like starlight, who gives a damn if they are alive or dead, they shine and that's that, and though in the daytime you can't see them but you know they are there.

So we won't hear that guitar anymore, and that's fine too, you can learn to get along without anything. God, how he could play. And when his hand didn't work anymore, he pulled down the blinds and kissed it all goodbye. To that, I've no objection. Sooner or later it happens, and it doesn't matter much how, anyway it has to happen, and who knows how many of us here this evening, ladies and gentlemen, will be alive in a month's time, certainly not everybody, it's statistically impossible. Someone who is pushing his neighbor or complaining because the person in front of him is blocking his view of the stage has already gone to the barber for the last time, but never mind, a year more or less doesn't make much difference, I don't feel bad for those who kick the bucket and I don't envy those who keep on going, nor do I care much to know what group I fall into.

Amen for Jerry, and for everybody and everything. As I said, I can't find fault with his decision, when someone wants to get off the bus, it's right to get off, and if he prefers to jump off while it's still moving, before the stop, that's his business. Someone can be fed up, tired, unable to take it anymore, what do I know. When seeing him down like that because he couldn't play as before, to cheer him up I told him that he had been one of the greats of the guitar, and he said that for him it wasn't enough to have been. He wanted to be—it didn't matter what, a musician, a lover, anything, but to be.

Yes, ladies and gentlemen, in that moment I

understood what great luck it is to be born like me, or to have an uncle or grandfather or whomever, born in Bratislava or Lwòw or Kaloea or in any other dump in this shabby Central Europe, which is a hell, a real cesspool. It's enough to smell that musty odor, that stink which is the same from Vienna to Czernowitz, but at least it doesn't force you to be, on the contrary. Yes, if Jerry had understood, when his hand didn't work anymore, his great luck in having been, the freedom, the vacation, the great privilege of not having to be anymore, of not having to play anymore, his free pass from the barracks of life!

But maybe he couldn't, since he wasn't born or raised in that stagnant Pannonian air, thick as a blanket, in that smoke-filled tavern where you eat badly and drink even worse, but are happy to be there when it's raining outside and the wind is howling—and outside, in life, it's always raining and the wind cuts through you. Yes, any grocer in Nitra or Varaždin could teach all of Fifth Avenue—except for those maybe who come from Nitra or Varaždin or some other place in those parts—the happiness of having been.

Oh, the modesty, the lightness of having been, that uncertain and accommodating space where everything is as light as a feather, against the presumption, the weight, the squalor, the freight of being! Please, I'm not talking about any kind of past and even less about nostalgia, which is stupid and hurtful, as the world itself says, nostalgia, the pain of returning. The past is horrific, we are barbaric and evil, but our grandparents and great-grandparents were even fiercer savages. I certainly wouldn't want to be, to live in their time. No, I'm saying that I would want to have always already been, exempt from the military service of existing. A slight disability is sometimes a way out, protecting you from the obligation of joining in and losing your skin.

Being hurts, it doesn't let up. Do this, do that, work, struggle, win, fall in love, be happy, you must be happy, living is this duty to be happy, if you're not how shameful. So, you do all you can to obey, to be as good and clever and happy as you ought, but how can you, things just fall on top of you, love smacks you on the head like a chunk of masonry off a roof, a wicked punch or worse. You walk hugging the walls to avoid those crazy cars, but the walls are crumbling, sharp rock and glass slicing your skin and making you bleed, you are in bed with someone and for an instant you understand what real life could and should be and it is an unbearable pang—picking your clothes off the floor, getting dressed, getting out and away. Luckily there's a bar nearby, how good a coffee or a beer tastes.

Yes, drinking a beer, for instance, is a way of having been. You're there, sitting down, you look at the foam evaporating, a little bubble every second, a heartbeat, one beat less, rest and the promise of rest for your tired heart; everything is behind you. I remember that my grandmother, when we went to visit her in Szabadka, would cover the sharp corners of the furniture with cloths and put away the iron table, so that we children wouldn't get hurt when we ran into something racing around the house, and she would even cover the electric plugs. To have been is this, living in this space where there are no sharp corners; you don't scrape your knee, you can't turn on the lamp that hurts your eyes, all is quiet, time out, no ambush.

So, ladies and gentlemen, this is the heritage that Central Europe has left us. A safe-deposit box, empty but with a lock on it to keep out bank robbers who might want to put who knows what inside it. Empty, nothing that grabs your heart and bites into your soul, life is there, already been, secure, safe from any accident, an out-of-circulation bank note for a hundred old crowns that you hang on the wall, under glass, with no fear of inflation. Even in a novel, the best part, at least for the writer, is the epilogue. Everything has already happened, been written, worked out; the characters live happily ever after or are dead, it's all the same, in any case nothing more can happen. The writer holds the epilogue in his hands, rereads it, maybe he changes a comma, but he runs no risk.

Every epilogue is happy, because it's an epilogue. You go out on the balcony, a breeze comes through the geraniums and the violets of thought, a drop of rain slides down your face; if it rains harder you like to listen to the drumming of the fat drops on the awning. When it stops you go take a little stroll, you exchange a few words with the neighbor you meet on the stairs; neither for him nor you does it matter what's said, it's just a pleasure to hesitate there a moment and from the window on the landing you can see way down there in the distance a strip of sea that the sun, now out from behind the clouds, lights up like a knife blade. Next week we're going to Florence, your neighbor says. O yes, it's nice, I've been there. And in this way you save yourself the fuss of traveling, the lines, the heat, the crowds, looking for a restaurant. A stroll in the evening air fresh with rain, then back home. You must not wear yourself out, otherwise you'll get too excited and sleep won't come. Insomnia, ladies and gentlemen, believe me, is a terrible thing. It crushes you, suffocates you, follows at your heels, chases you, poisons you—yes, insomnia is the supreme form of being—insomnia, that's why you have to sleep, sleeping is the only antechamber of the true having already been, but meanwhile it's already something, a sigh of relief . . .

Claudio Magris

STADELMANN

for my mother

DRAMATIS PERSONAE

Carl Wilhem Stadelmann, Goethe's ex-servant
Menz, Burgomaster's of Frankfurt's envoy
Warden of the poorhouse at Jena
Schramek, an inmate of the poorhouse
Körner, court optician and scientist
Steffi, laundress at the poorhouse
Madame Schnips, proprietress of a bordello
A Pimp
A Barber
A Postillion
Lori, a young woman
A Host
A Shadow
Schlosser, Goethe's relative
The Burgomaster of Frankfurt
Amalia Schoppe, actress
The Poorhouse Director
A Doctor
A Messenger
Goethe's voice
Old Inmates of the poorhouse, Scullery Maids, Washer-
    women, Prostitutes, Students, Councilmen and
    Dignitaries from Frankfurt, an Ecclesiastical Advisor,
    an Errand Boy, a Poorhouse Custodian, Waiters,
    Ladies, Knights

ACT I

SCENE 1

The stage is two-thirds invisible, engulfed in darkness. On the left a shining space, set off from the darkness as if by reflection. We see, on two small easels near the wall, two large cardboard sheets resting vertically, a white sheet with a black circle in the center and a black sheet with a white circle. A few yards to the right, almost at the edge of the darkness, a table where Stadelmann is working with pieces of carboard, scissors and glue. A couple of times he gets up and goes to the easels, carefully measuring with a compass the circles on the cardboard.

GOETHE'S VOICE: [*We only see the shadow of his caricatured profile, projected like a silhouette on the wall; the voice comes out of the darkness engulfing two-thirds of the stage.*] So, Stadelmann, are they equal? Perfectly equal, aren't they? All in due course, but without wasting any time. Come here, fine, just the right distance. [*Stadelmann turns back, he stops at the shadow's edge. Above*

him, high up, Goethe's silhouette.] Watch the two
circles carefully, like that, fine, again—What do
you see?

STADELMANN: What do you mean, what do I see?

GOETHE: [*impatient*] Look at the two circles! There,
like that, very good. So?

STADELMANN: But...the white one is bigger...[*we
see the white circle grow larger*]

GOETHE: Excellent, just like that! Exactly a fifth larger.
A dark object appears smaller than a light one of
the same dimension. Dark clothes make a person
look thinner, the crescent moon in conjunction
looks reduced by a fifth in respect to the same
crescent moon in opposition. Old Tycho Brahe
had already noticed that...

*Music. The two pieces of cardboard disappear,
in their place, a little higher up, in a play of lights,
we see a night sky with two white crescent moons
at first equal, one of them soon growing smaller
while the other enlarges, until they are superim-
posed in just one crescent, which then separates
and recomposes itself a few times, until finally
returning to the original scene.*

STADELMANN: But the circles are equal, I cut them myself. It's an illusion, a mistake of the senses...

GOETHE: The sense do not lie, Stadelmann, remember

that! If the Old Man had wanted us to see green or red and not those numbers of which mathematicians speak, he would know best why he did it. The two circles are equal, but to our eyes the light one seems bigger, there's no denying it. I will teach you a rule, Stadelmann, flying in the face of Newton and all his fanatics. Never scorn the senses, Stadelmann!

STADELMANN: Yeah, well, in this case I don't think Your Excellency has anything to worry about, in fact, just the other day, at the inn, Your Excellency had me—

GOETHE: Don't get carried away, Stadelmann. You know that I willingly close one eye, perhaps even two, in certain matters, which, after all, do not displease me in a young man, because he has the good sense and the good taste not to talk of them and not to give people cause to chatter.

STADELMANN: Well, I know how to clam up and those who in these matters keep opening their traps are those who, when push comes to shove, let a tidbit or two get away. I know the type well…

GOETHE [*continuing on his own*] Indeed, people are only interested in that, talking well above their heads, grabbing on to one's coattails, for the little that one lifts oneself above them, to get a better look—as it would please many gentlemen and ladies in Weimar, to know what we were up to, I and the Duke, in the woods and villages and in the shepard huts... Instead, they will never know any of it, the rest are things not worth mentioning. Rather, Stadelmann, do you recall when the girl came in?

STADELMANN: Do I remember? Who could forget that moment, Excellency? There, from that tavern door, in the shadows and in the dim glimmer of sunset, with that white face so luminous under her dark hair, and that red shawl, scarlet red.... I even permitted myself to write a few verses, and if Your Excellency would be so generous, as other times...

GOETHE: Yes, yes, Stadelmann, I know, you have a not inconsiderable talent, and, after all, each of us is capable of writing verses, even good ones... it is enough to study, apply oneself. Work, work...

STADELMANN: Certainly, certainly, but—who knows why, just to see the face of a woman like that and one feels like he's empty inside, somewhat happy but even very, well no, not sad, though—there, in that moment, Excellency, I remembered that once, as a child, I stayed behind in church after the others had gone, and I in there, with those candles, alone … and then that pure white breast we saw under the shawl …

GOETHE: We did not see any breast, Stadelmann, that inn is a proper place and that girl too. This is why I told you to let her be, when you wanted to follow her, indeed, to help her fetch water—you do, however, have a good memory for colors, I must admit, a well-practiced eye—black hair, white face and red shawl. When she stopped for an instant somewhat intimidated, she drew away quite bashfully, and against the background of the white wall in front of us we saw a black visage surrounded by a white glow, and a green colored dress.

STADELMANN: Yes, that image on the wall which disappeared so quickly, that red which became green and that face which gleamed black like coal in a fire and the fair hair full of light, for just a second or so … why just a second or so? The morning is always so dark when I get up … Yes, I would have told her right away, in that instant there against the wall, to stop, even if—

GOETHE: Leave that Faust alone now, Stadelmann, it's already enough if I understand something of this—let's get back to work, take that black figure, there, and that gray cardboard …

The light goes out, the whole scene sinks into darkness.

SCENE 2

The entire stage is lit. A squalid room, the parlor in the poorhouse at Jena; some benches, a table, windows that look like blind eyes, on the wall a portrait of the Grand Duke and Grand Duchess of Saxony-Weimar. Stadelmann is on his feet, twisting and turning a beret in his hands, his gaze distracted and far off. In respect to the previous scene, he is naturally much older; a little past sixty, tall and thin, vigorous but worn and shabby. He puts on a faded dress-coat, under which we see a vest with a yellow border. Near him the supervising inspector and Menz, just arrived from Frankfurt on behalf of the burgomaster. Behind the door some old inmates from the poorhouse, curiously looking on.

STADELMANN: [*staring at nothing, still lost in his memories*] Yes, as I was saying, he was more attached to his theories on color than to his poetry, I know more than a little about this, instead of these professors nowadays—

WARDEN: Fine, fine, but we have already heard the

story, Stadelmann, Mr. Menz didn't come all the way from Frankfurt to learn it all by heart too.

OLD MAN: [*outside the door*] He's somebody from Frankfurt, who knows what he's doing here.

ANOTHER OLD MAN: Maybe to nab him, for some filth from thirty years ago. As far as I'm concerned—

MENZ: It is actually because we know you have so many memories, so many things to tell us, that the burgomaster thought, on this auspicious occasion...

A THIRD OLD MAN: Did you see last night Kunz did it all over himself? Maybe now they want me to be the one to clean up his shit.

FIRST OLD MAN: Seems like even this year, at Christmas, there's going to be goose. Heavens, goose, a little piece, but—anyway let's see, a week, two, three, no, wait, today is—good God, what are they talking about?

STADELMANN: [*almost an aside*] You need to have seen those colors, as I saw them myself—but who's going to see them now, without him who will show them to me and explain them... [*he pulls a thread from his beret and keeps looking at it*]

MENZ: It will be a grand festival, worthy of Germany's greatest poet and the noble, free imperial city that gave him birth.

WARDEN: Put that beret down somewhere, Stadelmann.

STADELMANN: [*he shakes himself and turns to Menz, adopting a different tone*] Even I, in his time, helped him discover a couple of little things that not even he, without me, would have ... do you know, one time, at dinner, there was a wonderful bottle, yes, an Eilfer '11, the wine of the century, he used to call it, who knew all about it, as I, when it comes to the rest ... anyway, I was saying, that night ...

MENZ: Interesting, very interesting, of course, all that concerns Goethe is very interesting. You will see how delighted they will be to listen to this story in Frankfurt, to hear one of the few who knew Goethe and who, after so many years, is still—

STADELMANN: Yes, one of the few, in every way. Already then, regardless ...

OLD MAN: So who wants to listen? and about what?

ANOTHER OLD MAN: A festival? And he's going to be invited, him?

THIRD OLD MAN: Sure, it will always be that same old story, when he used to live with his great poet, we know.

MENZ: You will see what a beautiful monument. I will bring great satisfaction even to you, to everyone.

STADELMANN: Yes, of course, if they feel like listening to me, I'll have some good ones to tell—it's always that, looking at those ladies and gentlemen in the face, you see it's worth it, because, you know, everybody's capable of sitting there listening to a good story, but...

WARDEN: Stadelmann...

MENZ: But?

STADELMANN: But, but...there, how can I say, a monument would be fine, that's understood, in fact, it's necessary, but he was a lot more than a monument! Sometimes he'd come along with so brusque a manner that even the soldiers who were part of the Duke's own escort would stop dead in their tracks...other times he looked like a devil, who you grab hold of here and he jumps out over there...

WARDEN: Standelmann, now don't you begin—

MENZ: But no, no, in fact, some previously unknown episode from the life of the poet would be much more desirable, most desirable, a new example of his greatness, of his noble humanity...

Raising this highly prized monument, the city
intends actually—

STADELMANN: Yes, he also knew he was a monument,
sure, very intimidating and serious in not saying
anything or just saying some banality that made
you embarrassed anyway . . . Sometimes it seemed
that, of the two of us, I was the monument . . . yes,
I ran up and down for him the whole day long,
but always the same and capable in my place, like
a statue . . . Even if sometimes—Yes, of course, of
course, you will see that I won't embarrass you,
in fact, in fact, I am quite honored by your trust,
and I hope . . .

MENZ: Certainly, all will go quite well and, keeping
in mind the particular circumstances, and the
opportunity and the suitability . . .

STADELMANN: I lived for eight years with His Excellency, didn't I? I wrote his diary, even letters and
all in all . . . Now you see me like this, in this . . . but
once . . . even his books . . . [*joyfully*] anyway tell the
burgomaster that he will not regret the consider-
ation that he has seen fit to show me.

OLD MAN: I knew that sooner or later he'd begin telling
some tall ones!

WARDEN: Don't give yourself so many airs, Stadelmann,
you're only lucky that Professor Riemer is sick, or

else no one would have remembered you. It is only because he can't come that they invited you.

STADELMANN: If you think that I feel bad...as if I didn't know, after so many years of living with him, that everybody is just taking the place of somebody else...

OLD MAN: Now he's just getting going—you'll see—

WARDEN: Instead of all this chattering, go get your things ready, perhaps best to leave the bottle under your bed, in that lovely little hiding place of yours...

MENZ [*embarrassed*]: Ah, yes, as we were saying a moment ago with the Director, I would just like to suggest, even if perhaps I know it isn't really necessary...

STADELMANN: I understand, Mr. Metz, don't worry. Even if, in homage to him, who drank two bottles a day—

WARDEN: Remember your place, Stadelmann!

STADELMANN: Most willingly, if I knew what it was...

WARDEN: A place in the poorhouse, you know this better than I, and you can thank heaven even for this.

MENZ: It isn't worthwhile, certainly now that I have had the pleasure to make personal contact, according

to the burgomaster's wishes, as Mr. Stadelmann
seems in condition to come to Frankfurt...I mean,
health condition, you understand, because—in
as much as the caring and faithful servant of the
poet...

WARDEN: Ex-servant, to be precise.

STADELMANN: Everyone is an ex-, ex I don't know
what, so many aren't even aware.

OLD MAN: [*outside the door*] At least he has the con-
solation not to be an ex-drunkard, certainly not
that...

ANOTHER OLD MAN: Shut up, if only everybody in
here was like him—

STADELMANN: [*without paying the others any mind*]
Ex, ex, ex everything...I at least was aware of
whose service I was in, whom I went up and
down all day for...while he, even he knew himself just to be at the service of someone, a tunic
with many grand decorations, but he didn't know
from whom...sometimes, when I used to see him
wandering around in the room of busts, between
Venus's statue and that of Schiller, it seemed that
I was looking at an empty dressing gown or a set
of tails, floating in the air...

MENZ: [*fidgety*] Well, in Frankfurt we will have the
opportunity to go over the program, what to say

to the public, a select and exclusive public…and you, as the poet's witness, as a faithful mirror, if I may say so—

STADELMANN: No, not exactly a mirror, Mr. Menz. No, I was not his true and duplicate copy, as was said of Seidel, who was in his service for many years before me and walked like him, shook his head like him, wrote like him…and of course, he became rich, a true, respectable bourgeois gentleman, while I—and then he even ended up in an asylum, he didn't say a word, he wasn't even aware of people coming close to him…

WARDEN: [*aside*] Or else he might have been a sponger too.

STADELMANN: [*going on distracted*]…who knows, maybe in his urge to resemble him he ended up being like him, a mask without anything inside, and when he realized it, it was too late, he was already completely empty, a scarecrow in a garden, in the asylum's garden…

WARDEN: This is truly…if it were up to me, I…

MENZ: What a sad story, truly tragic…ah, life, sometimes…And then, a great poet's destiny…

STADELMANN: [*paying no attention*]…sure, His Excellency had the strength to be nothing, but the others who followed him were not up to it, I knew that right away, and I resisted him, by God I resisted him so that he wouldn't pull me down, so I wouldn't be like him, besides the famous two bottles a day I once in a while drank a third, maybe even a fourth, if I could—and then, sure, I felt good, when I got sleepy and felt myself growing nice and heavy, even if I had to go around taking care of things, putting things away, cleaning, copying, keeping the accounts, lighting and putting out the candles, up and down until one in the morning... but I was all nice and heavy, like when we're sitting in the summer lifting our heads towards the hot hot sun, and the world is red like behind our shut eyelids, like His Excellency's colored shadows, like wine... and when I felt a belch coming I felt like somebody, I felt like Stadelmann...

WARDEN: Certainly you must have been drinking again, shame on you! Please, do not fear, Menz, I know all to well, you will see—

MENZ: Farewell until Frankfurt, Stadelmann, and don't forget, all of you don't forget...

He moves towards the door and the lights go out.

SCENE 3

In the poorhouse dormitory. Stadelmann is alone, sitting on a bed.

STADELMANN: Look, who would imagine, after so many years, who would've still thought...of course it entered my mind, but I didn't want these people here to see anything [*he glances around at the other beds in the dormitory*] I didn't want to tell them anything, just something every once in a while, just to egg them on a little—Now if they realize...

Let's see now, first I have to take care of that wood in the garden, then I have to say goodbye, you know, then I have to get my stuff ready, and then— [*he gets off the bed and moves toward the door*]

Of course there's...

SCENE 4

In the poorhouse garden, barren and empty. It's winter. Stadelmann and Schramek—an old man more or less his age, without a leg—are cutting pieces of wood, blowing on their hands because of the cold. They put on badly patched work clothes; Schramek every once in a while pulls a flask out of his pocket and takes a swig.

STADELMANN: Come on, there, hold the wood straight.

SCHRAMEK: Why do you give a damn if it's straight? Are you trying to look good or do you feel you have to earn that warmed-over shit they feed you every night at supper? You're better off having a swig.

STADELMANN: No, thanks, not now.

SCHRAMEK: Yeah, I forgot, we're getting ready to play the gentleman in Frankfurt.

STADELMANN: Please, let's go a little faster.

SCHRAMEK: What's all the hurry? The stage coach isn't here yet, there are still a few days left, right, why all the fuss... Maybe it's better in there? With this here [*he drinks from the flask*] I feel warmer than sitting next to the stove.

STADELMANN: Hand me the ax.

SHRAMEK: Right away, wait a minute... look what a nice blade, a little dull maybe, but... whack! And these rust spots—maybe it's blood, who knows what…When at Leipzig that ball shattered my leg, I saw blood running out of me everyplace, lots of blood, and I was thinking that if somebody had given me a barrel of wine to drink chugging it down without taking a breath, glug glug glug, as much wine down my throat as blood was pouring out my thigh, I was thinking that I wouldn't die, and I was thinking of the wine, that red, I was thinking…even if those who put me on the stretcher told me, later, that before passing out I was screaming and screaming loud, the hell with thinking—

STADELMANN: Let's go, give it here.

SCHRAMEK: A little patience, mister secret servant to the counselor, no, servant to the secret counselor…I don't have many other toys, be good to this poor good little boy, let him play—You know, from when they cut my leg off, at Leipzig, with a thing that wasn't much different, I became quite fond of these gizmos…whack, the tree falls and the leg goes off on its own, if we could cut the earth in two, nice and round as it is, slice it like a watermelon and make so much red juice come out…see how good this dark red stain looks on the iron, how this dirty spot shines…

STADELMANN: You always drag out these things, you repeat each time that horrible scene...I understand that for you...but—

SCHRAMEK: Yeah, we know, you prefer instead to talk always about those bonfires that you saw just a year later, on the anniversary [*emphatic*] of our glorious victory at Leipzig over the French—[*striking his thigh*] and of this little souvenir that those French left me. All those fires on the hillsides must have been beautiful, right? Even those hillsides were nice and red, but with grape vines, right? Ah, yes, it was October, like the year before...

STADELMANN: What an unforgettable October...I was the first to read his poems for Marianne, those oriental verses...

SCHRAMEK: [*striking his wooden leg again*] Unforgettable for me too, sure, truly unique...it must have been a really beautiful show that night, seeing the bonfires from that little place in the vineyard, with your Counselor and his chick twittering and rubbing against each other in the dark, and the happy cuckold looking the other way and you sitting even admiring the scene and what your Excellency was enjoying, not that you could've done anything else anyway...always better in any case than lying on the ground in a lake of blood like me, just the October before.

STADELMANN: Look, if you think I don't understand…

SCHRAMEK: Sure, you truly understand and feel very sorry, but about these things, like legs cut off, that one taught you not to speak, right? It's not good manners, even you wrinkle your nose when I open my mouth, just as those gentlemen who wrinkle theirs when it's you who's babbling on or when, unlike today, it's this [*lifting the bottle*] you suck on a little too much yourself.—Come on, drink up!

STADELMANN: I already told you I don't feel like it.

SCHRAMEK: For what it might do for you now… you might have been a little more scrupulous before. So that Your Excellency wouldn't have tossed you out.

STADELMANN: It wasn't because of that… not only for that. And it wasn't for the bookkeeping, where I even bothered to record the pennies for a candle, as he had taught me. Then when Doctor Weller made clear that everything was in order, very much in order, he was quite pleased and flattered that I—

SCHRAMEK: But he still fired you. Gentlemen's mysteries. We instead can't fire anybody, we can't say to the superintendent congratulations mister inspector, you are terrific but I do not find your face pleasing today, my planets are not in alignment, there are your references, now get going, with all my best wishes and good luck. If I could only fire myself, throw myself out of this lousy poorhouse...

STADELMANN: Yes, he didn't waste any time getting rid of obstacles, he let go of people like you take off a shirt or a pair of shoes... even little Ulrike, for whom he did a lot of crazy things and was ready to do some even crazier, a few weeks later he barely remembered her.

SCHRAMEK: Well, he was right when it came to women, it's what you have to do.

STADELMANN: You know what he said, at that dinner in honor of that Polish beauty? [*gesturing as if making a toast*] "I don't admit to memory, there is no past of which to be nostalgic, everything is always eternally new!" But if I think about myself, about my life, it seems as if there was never anything new...

SCHRAMEK: [*striking his leg*] For me, instead, this was a true novelty.

STADELMANN: Maybe that's why I forget nothing...

SCHRAMEK: Yeah, well, I forget everything.

STADELMANN: And I nothing...and sometimes it's so confusing that I'm almost dizzy...even if I think of Frankfurt, I don't know what to say, what to do...

SCHRAMEK: A great big fart, Carl, in everybody's face, like the trumpet on Judgment Day. Anyway, with the wind that blows in those parts, in a second you won't even hear that sigh... [*he hits the bottle again, Stadelmann goes back inside*]

SCENE 5

The court optician and scientist Körner's laboratory. Instruments, glass plates, all kinds of lenses scattered here and there. Körner is an elderly though solid man; he talks slowly in a pedantic way. Stadelmann stays near him, following with a slightly embarrassed air, while the other keeps bustling around.

KÖRNER: Fine, fine, Stadelmann, congratulations, I am pleased. A very fine satisfaction. Mind you now...

STADELMANN: So, Doctor, not—

KÖRNER: Very well, how touchy you are. If there's someone who has demonstrated his respect for

you, who put his trust in you, who for years of-
fered you work, it was I, wasn't it? Certainly it's
not my fault if then—

STADELMANN: I know I know, it was my fault—[*he
picks up a piece of glass*] what a beautiful piece
of leaded glass, exactly like those he used to like
so much...

KÖRNER: Yes, the Counselor, he used to always turn
to me, I must say, for those experiments of
his...most, most interesting. When he needed
a lens, a filter—

STADELMANN: I made lots of them, tinted glass like
this...

KÖRNER: And you broke as many more, that time,
after that squabble with Kunz, another rascal
that one...I used to tell you, I always told you
Stadelmann, one glass does you good, two do
nothing, three—

STADELMANN: I know that ditty too, it's on all the
farmer's almanacs.

KÖRNER: Well, it's water under the bridge...I hope.
Who knows what had gotten into you in those
days...yes, I understand, the sorrow for the loss
of that poor soul, but there are ways and there
are ways—

STADELMANN: Sorrow?

KÖRNER: [*shocked*] I am talking about poor Rosine-Marie, God bless her, that sainted wife of yours who had so many trials and tribulations…

STADELMANN: Yes, she had many trials, yes…

KÖRNER: It was after her death, just ten years ago, that you began letting yourself go, good Lord began, not as if before…yet…in as much as I myself, heartsick, though appreciating your talents, at a certain point I had to, I couldn't do any less, after the umpteenth time…

STADELMANN: [*aside*] Rosine-Marie…sure, just ten years, yet…I who was saying that I forget nothing…she was blond, once, and certainly when I first knew her in her father's shop she didn't have that face that was so tired, but—sleeping, getting up, going back to bed at night, for twenty-three years…and that pillow that always ended up on the ground, that was in the beginning or…

KÖRNER: She truly was an angel. When she had that wicked fever, and you were on a trip with the Counsellor, I was happy to be able to help her and she, poor thing, always used to say that I had saved her life…ah, what an angel.

STADELMANN: Yes, she had that terrible fever, it's true…

KÖRNER: Well, what a great satisfaction it would be

for her too, now, in Frankfurt…Do it for her as
well, this trip, and mind you, no silliness, you
know how heartsick she would get when you,
every now and then—

STADELMANN: Yes, yes… [*energetically*] Doctor, I
thank you. Farewell.

KÖRNER: Then you will tell me how it went, I am very
curious about—

STADELMANN: Of course, of course. [*moving off*]
Farewell, Doctor Körner.

SCENE 6

*In the poorhouse laundry, a kind of barn beyond the
garden. Clothes, sheets, washtubs, dirt-stained linens.
Steffi, next to Stadelmann, is rinsing clothes; she is a
middle-aged woman, grown heavy and faded, but with
a hearty and vital bearing that allows one to see her
former beauty. Next to the two of them appear and slip
away some female figures, at once real—today's and
yesterday's washerwomen and scullery maids—and
imaginary, evoked by Stadelmann's fantasy.*

STADELMANN: So then, Steffi.

STEFFI: Well, look who's here. If it wasn't that I've

known for ages a pair of beat-up britches that end up in my tub every once in a while, flying in the face of regulations, I would've said that you had finally kicked the bucket.

STADELMANN: A little patience, still just a very little…sure, excuse me for the pants, I know we're not supposed to, but since Lisa, when she comes to clean up the parlor, is always saying that she's sure that you, tell me if not—anyway I was thinking…

STEFFI: A leopard changes its spots and even its vices but men, I see, don't ever loose that tone, yes, that tone like after screwing…ah how well I know this innocent chatter, the air of someone begging pardon while he's already putting his shoes on, not even five minutes after the little deed…

STADELMANN: [*circling her waist*] These little deeds are so horrible, are they? God what thighs, but for you time never passes, I must say, you must have made a bargain with the Devil, a real Faust in a skirt and I'm the poodle dog, the Devil's poodle, bow wow [*he hugs her pretending he is biting*]

STEFFI: [*pulling away, but not too far*] Here we chase dogs out with a broom…drop it, silly, because then I'd like to see, if we get to that point—O you really are—

43

STADELMANN: [*suddenly changes tone and rests his head on her shoulder, gently caressing her back*] I'd like to sleep, Steffi, I'm not kidding, I mean just sleep, here with you ... because going to Frankfurt, what then? ...

STEFFI: Yes, I've heard the story. Well, just like always, you've come to see me to say goodbye, you think of me only when you're getting ready to take off for someplace else.

STADELMANN: Yes, exactly, I mean, no, I wanted to say that I'm going there, and then coming back here, and ... now that I think about it, all that traveling, all those people, who knows all those new faces ... it would be wonderful instead to go to your house, to your house from the old days, at the end of the lane, remember ...

STEFFI: It's odd that you remember it ... you were in such a hurry to leave that time ... Go ahead, go to Frankfurt, the trip is not as long—

Lights go out, all is dark. After a very brief pause the lights come up on a space a little more to the left and towards the rear. It's a kitchen, Stadelmann—younger—is seated and two girls are each bringing him a beer.

STADELMANN: After they had already played the second serenade, that one says: hey, you're not getting any funny ideas in your head, you're not thinking of taking any liberties with me? I am the daughter of the postmaster.

Everyone laughs. Stadelmann picks up the beers and crossing his arms drinks one then the other, then circles the waists of the two girls, still with the beer mugs in hand he tries to get them closer to his mouth, sticking his head between the two girls, who are laughing and screeching.

Ah what beer, this one's better, no, that one, but look I'm not squeezing, I'm just trying to drink, right? But why is life so hard? [*The girls are writhing*]

ONE GIRL: Let us work, we still have to—

STADELMANN: Only if you give me a kiss, a kiss for each beer and a beer for each kiss…

THE OTHER GIRL: There! [*She takes his beer and moves it to her lips, kissing the other side of the mug*]

STADELMANN: It's a trick, a cheat, I'll take it up with your boyfriend!

STEFFI: [*she enters the kitchen, the girls pull away and Stadelmann stands up*] May I or do I need an invitation?

STADELMANN: [*he takes a long, serious look at her*] Pardon me, my name is Stadelmann, Carl Wilhelm Stadelmann…

The two look at each other, the girls have drawn back. The lights go out. When they come back up, they light the previous space on the right, the poorhouse laundry.

STEFFI: Yes, I recall exactly how you said it, Carl Wilhelm Stadelmann…

STADELMANN: I recall exactly how you entered, that red kerchief around your neck, haughty, and those eyes black as coals, how they were looking at me in a way, in a way…

Lights go out, coming back up lighting an area even more to the left, towards the back. An interior, a bed; outside it is night.

STADELMANN: I love you, Steffi.

STEFFI: It's not true, but it doesn't matter. It's me that loves you.

Lights out; then they come back up on the original scene in the laundry.

STEFFI: In fact it was exactly like that. [*she keeps rinsing clothes*]

STADELMANN: No, believe me, it's not true, it's hard to explain but I truly—I know it seems ridiculous, seeing that not much later, when you—though you have to understand that even you—

STEFFI: It doesn't matter, I got over it quick. Then I had some fun too. You were a handsome man, you had you peculiarities, half bumbling half sly, like all men, you even knew how to make me laugh—even after—so what more do you want? And now…

STADELMANN: [*passionately*] Yes, you're right, I was terrible but I loved you, Steffi, you know it too…when you used to laugh throwing back your hair and your throat, that big, white throat that pulled me under like a river…and your breasts like moons, that chestnut down on your arms…[*he takes her hands and kisses them*] What big, strong hands, but why…?

STEFFI: I'd really like to know too, actually I should be the one asking you, don't you think, because…[*she begins singing softly and rinsing clothes*] you-know-how-it-goes-we-never-know-why-then-it-happens-and-we-ask-alas-but-who-knows-why-who-ever-knows-why…

Lights go out, and in the dark we still hear this ditty that little by little, from the whisper of before, takes on a coarse tone. Lights go back up illuminating the left part of the stage toward the rear. It is Madame Schnips' bordello: sofa, pillows on the floor, some girls in the background, one brashly singing the song. Little by little the scene becomes even more phantasmagoric.

MADAME SCHNIPS: Come now! Don't you recognize me? Much admired and reviled, I, Helen... [*laughs*] Entrez, please, this is a small way station for travelers who suffer from nostalgia. A small remedy for a grand sickness, the gentleman will say, but an effective remedy...

STADELMANN: [*he takes a few steps, looking around*] And yet I would've sworn...

A GIRL: [*she comes close brushing against him*] Here we don't swear...

STADELMANN: That one over there, with two breasts like moons...and that other back there—stop, wait!

In the background we make out female figures, making gestures of beckoning and fleeing, covering and uncovering themselves.

ANOTHER GIRL: [*who looks like Steffi*] I was sure that you would come back in the end—

STADELMANN: What do you mean, come back? But I haven't—

THE GIRL: It's late, how much time...

STADELMANN: Much time? But I've always been here— [*he looks at her*] It's impossible, Steffi, it can't be, it wasn't my fault...how could you have—

THE GIRL: [*backing away*] 'Women, used to the love of menfolk,/ Not the choosers look to be,/ But the

48

cunning judges;/ That's a right they claim as well/ Upon the upright members'… [*cabaret music*]

MADAME SCHNIPS: Did you hear? If the poet says it…

STADELMANN: Damn the poet! Steffi, where are you? This is good for me too, it's so nice here, why are leaving…

CHORUS OF GIRLS: 'Admit, we one and all are/ Captive here, as we have often been/ Since the Trojan's inglorious/ Overthrow, and the fearful/ Labyrinthine journey's woes'…

MADAME SCHNIPS: [*she claps her hands*] Here, all of you, good girls, slaves of your masters…

The girls come and wrap themselves around Stadelmann, hugging him.

STADELMANN: I would like…

MADAME SCHNIPS: I would like the grass not even to be greener in the king's garden, didn't they teach you that, sniveler? Or do we have to teach you with a good spanking? Take what you find on your plate and thank the Lord for a nice piece of meat.

STADELMANN: But I was looking for her, the one…the one with the red kerchief, dark eyes—

MADAME SCHNIPS: I see we need to teach our little gentleman his ABC's. Red kerchief or dark eyes [*pointing to one after another of the girls*] Merchandise for every taste: long legs, budding breasts, melon breasts, here there's a big ass, here a mouth like a pump... But none of us have a clue who you're talking about, what is she? If you want a ~~pair of nice buns, or two big creamy tits, it would~~ be a lot easier.

STADELMANN: Yes, it's true, everything a lot easier... [*he grabs and touches the girls, who are all over him*] tits, legs, that foot... no, you're not getting away! [*he throws himself on the bed among the pile of girls, trying to grab a foot frolicking among the pillows and blankets*]

MADAME SCHNIPS: So sink! And I can also say: rise up!

Enters a kind of pimp, who looks like the Superintendent.

PIMP: The poorhouse is not a bordello and the bordello is not a poorhouse, we are not giving out charity here! I'm going to throw you out, you drunken whoremonger!

GOETHE'S SILHOUETTE AND VOICE: I am waiting, Stadelmann [*the silhouette disappears*]

STADELMANN: [*he sits up on the bed, while the girls move into the background*] Yes, Excellency, I know, it's already four-thirty, I know it's time to get up,

I'm coming, but I went to bed at one, yes, I'm getting up now, you'll see that everything will be in order, even the accounts will balance, it's just that those numbers confused me a little if I could only stay in bed another half-hour, I'm sure if Your Excellency had a look at these girls you would as always understand...

GOETHE'S SILHOUETTE AND VOICE: [*for a moment, as before*] Even my patience has its limits and when it is necessary to break off a rapport with annoying persons, unfortunately even harshly—

STADELMANN: I won't do it again, Excellency, not even a drop—[*he pulls a bottle out from under the bed and holds it out towards the empty stage*] Why is it so easy to slip up, for a poor devil like me!

GOETHE'S SILHOUETTE AND VOICE: [*as before*] As long as a man toils he is subject to error, but in his dark instinct a good man will always know the true path.

STADELMANN: Yes, and then it all bursts like a soap bubble and goodbye beautiful colors...

PIMP: Your stay is over, out!

THE GIRL WHO LOOKS LIKE STEFFI: Don't go, nobody has the right to send you away, don't leave [*she disappears*]

STADELMANN: [*standing*] No, I really have to leave

now, I haven't even gotten my things together [*he moves towards the exit*]

CHORUS OF GIRLS: 'What can this be?/ sisters, see what comes! Had we not jocund bright day?/ Who bids us, commands us that we return/ To the cheerlessness of the gray glimmering/ Filled with beings insubstantial'…[*Lights out. They come back up, lighting the laundry*]

STEFFI: [*she makes a soap bubble with the laundry water*] Do you still like to play with soap bubbles?

STADELMANN: Listen, Steffi…so then I'll be seeing you when I get back, I'll tell you all about—

STEFFI: If it was up to me, I wouldn't go to all this trouble. I don't know why you're making such a fuss, it isn't like you're going to America…

SCENE 7

In the poorhouse Stadelmann is sitting on a chair and the barber is just finishing with his beard and hair.

BARBER: There, like this, great, now you are ready for Frankfurt. It's the first time somebody from the poorhouse is invited among the gentry and so even we have to work miracles.

STADELMANN: [*looking in the mirror, very pleased*] And so—

BARBER: Yeah, well, this is nothing, you ought to see what I can do with corpses, how I make them just right for the funerals. A month ago they called me to work on somebody who drowned. I can't tell you how the face was all swollen, he'd been in the water for three days. So, with a little cream, scissors, razor, etc., I fixed him up so that he was a pleasure to look at, handsome, plump, calm, he looked like he was asleep…

STADELMANN: [*aside*] One hell of an undertaker … [*looking again in the mirror*] Congratulations, excellent—my God, with this face here, not bad at all, I've got to say, maybe even I had a little something to do with it—

BARBER: A lot less than you think. It seems you don't know what a barber really is. Sure, in your place here, they never call on me, neither for the living nor the dead, except for this special occasion [*he adds some final touches with scissors and brush*] Look, a face, in itself it's not much … [*he taps him a few times on the cheeks*]

STADELMANN: Hey, boss, what do you mean, not much?

BARBER: Yes sir, just like I said. Take a face in the morning, with all those bags under swollen eyes...or somebody's face with stomach trouble, or who got completely plastered, or who'd been working like a dog all day...so what is it? Nothing. Who makes it into something, a real face? The barber. The barber is a sculptor, he cuts, shortens, stretches, rounds off... When I'm working on somebody like you now, do you know what I'm thinking? That I'm working on a funeral mask.

STADELMANN: Same to you—[*touching his testicles to ward off bad luck*]

BARBER: Do you know why? Because people, at any given moment, always have either a tired face or a happy or sad or angry one, in short, a temporary face. Instead, between beard, hair, pimples, nose hairs, etc., we pull out of it the ideal face, good for all occasions and uses. A classic face, I dare say to you who had the privilege to know up close our most supreme, classic poet. Have you ever noticed how all those fine, ancient statues look like manikins. And what is a funeral mask if not a face good for all eternity? [*brushing him one last time*] Exactly like yours, now.

STADELMANN: What the hell kind of hex... [*he stands up a little annoyed*] Well, alright...so, yes, thank you—

BARBER: Just doing my duty. You will see. I'm telling you, you'll see... [*exits*]

SCENE 8

In the poorhouse dormitory Stadelmann is getting ready for his trip, pulling out some things from a small pile on his bed. Next to the other beds, a few old men who watch.

STADELMANN: [*mumbling to himself, rummaging*] This yes, nobody's going to take a smoke away from me, not even he, who couldn't stand tobacco, was able to get me to stop this nasty habit... [*pulls out his pipe*] This scarf, no, it's too ragged but what ever happened to my gloves. They still fit? [*he finds two or three apples while turning his things upside down*] There... [*holding an apple out to his neighbor*] Want it?

OLD MAN: So, that's where that rotten smell was coming from.

ANOTHER: Stick it... what are you up to now, giving us charity, acting like a gentleman?

A THIRD: What a bunch of silly old mummies... pass them over here. [*bites into one*] Thanks, Carl.

FIRST OLD MAN: And that, what's that?

STADELMANN: Ah, his coat and tails, still in good shape when he gave them to me [*he turns the coat around, showing the others and looking at it carefully*] Not bad, presenting me up there in that beautiful place with his coat and tails...look here, see these spots? [*pointing to the coat near the lapels*] Here were his decorations, he used to wear them all together, Napoleon's Legion of Honor, the Order of St. Anne given him by the Czar, and Leopold's, which he received from the Austrian Emperor...He was so fond of them! He used to say that they weren't much, but such worthless old coins might help shield him against some inconvenient...

SECOND OLD MAN: How could it be, they we all butchering each other but they each gave him a medal and he wore them all together?

STADELMANN: Yes, yes, they were whining to him about it, and he didn't give a damn, he was able to spend time with you and with your enemy, with everyone and no one... [*looking at the spots*] Who knows if they will give me a medal too to pin here? Certainly, with a handsome thing like this, maybe—[*putting the coat and tails aside*]

THIRD OLD MAN: Know what? You ought to swap

invitations and have the burgomaster and all those gentlemen and ladies come here, we'll figure out how to throw them a nice little party… [*the others laugh*]

FIRST OLD MAN: Have they told you where they're putting you up, in a real hotel, with breakfast in your room?

STADELMANN: I don't know, I don't have any idea, I think that…

SECOND OLD MAN: And that, what's that?

STADELMANN: [*picking up a rock*] This? It's a piece of granite, which I found on the Main during that trip… sure, just thirty years ago. There were only a few times I saw him as happy as that, when I spied this thing and bang, I jumped down from the box, grabbed it and he put out his hand from the coach window: magnificent stone, my lad, you truly have an eagle eye…

THIRD OLD MAN: Was he really fond of that stuff?

STADELMANN: God knows he liked minerals, rocks, shells, we never stopped collecting them, to take them home, arranging them in boxes, cases, display cases, glass cupboards… [*looks at the room's bare walls*] Here instead there's nothing, and somebody because of seeing only empty walls, ends up looking at them as you look at a mirror, and thinking too much about himself... fossils, minerals, all those animal skulls and skeletons, the herbarium, succulents, knick knacks, cameos, prints, plaster casts... he knew so well not to look within, like that night I was standing there completely befuddled with staring into the void and he came up to me without making a sound, put his hand on my shoulder and said to me: turn your head the other way, Stadelmann, always try to look at the world... [*Two or three other old men enter, including Schramek*]

AN OLD MAN: Try on these shoes, maybe they're a little small but for a few days...

ANOTHER: [*a little goofy but with his hat in hand*] A hat is needed, you need a hat. But why do you need a hat, where do you have to go?

A THIRD: [*tearing the hat from the other man's hand*] Give it here, moron. [*sticks it on Stadelmann's head*] It doesn't look good on you, understand, but do you want that a gentleman's hat should look good on you? As far as I'm concerned they'll stick it up your ass, one way or another.

SECOND OLD MAN: [*one of the first*] Yes, yes, so he's going to Frankfurt, that way he'll wear even those people out with all his stories, Counselor here,

Excellency there, we're fed up with it, who does he think he is…

AN OLD MAN: [*the one who came in with the hat*] What sausages, who has the sausages…

STADELMANN: Thank you, thank you.

SCHRAMEK: This to keep you company, you never know [*gives him a bottle, which Stadelmann mechanically slips away in his coat pocket*]

WARDEN: [*enters with a pair of trousers in hand which he places on Stadelmann's arm*] Here, the Director says that you can't go around with your pants falling down like this, and have everyone laughing at the poorhouse… Hurry up, the coach will be by soon [*exits*]

THE OLD MEN: Have a good trip, Carl, farewell! [*they exit*]

Stadelmann stands still, hat on his head, trousers on his arm and shoes in hand. Curtain.

ACT II

SCENE 1

Stadelmann en route on the stagecoach; he is sitting up on the box, next to the postiliion, gesticulating excitedly.

A VOICE FROM INSIDE THE COACH: Come down, you'll have a fit, with all that wind up there!

STADELMANN: [*turning and lowering his head towards the coach window*] No, thank you, I prefer to stay up here, like in the old days…no, there isn't too much wind, and besides there is this to consider [*he pulls the bottle out of his coat*] yes, yes, I know, please don't worry…what good fresh air, it's not even dusty up here…

POSTILLION: Lucky you that you don't mind it, I'm already feeling it all over me—sure, traveling for you all seems a big deal, like this every once in a while, but when you have to climb up here every morning and then be away all day just looking at a road, you realize that traveling only gets you a bad stomach and you see nothing, just curves to the right and then to the left...Ho! [*yells at the horses*]

STADELMANN: Damn, they run hard...what light on those fields down there, it doesn't even feel like winter...and the clouds up here...he was right, how beautiful the world is and grand...it's true that because of always being in there for so many years, you—Are we going to cross that wood there or are we cutting to the right?

POSTILLION: Yeah, sure, to the right, don't you see there is no road through the wood...in the poorhouse, how do you get along?

STADELMANN: Who gives a damn about the poorhouse, let it fall apart...It's getting cold [*he drinks*] What a wind, never saw a wind like this, and what a day—so clear, shining, far away...Who knows what that town is down there...Want some [*holding out the bottle*]

POSTILLION: Thanks [*drinks*] Very good.

VOICE FROM THE ROAD: Good day, Doctor!

STADELMANN: What Doctor? Oh, I see, it's because of the hat, but that's alright anyway, good day, good day! [*he bares his head*] A hat like this is a real doctor, *Doctor juris,* answer, Doctor, you must deign to reply! Anyway, when they take off the hat, it's never for us, for none of us, he knew it too when they said Excellency to him they weren't really bowing to him, to the son of Madame Aja... We too are like those sheets of his paper, that look red or blue to us because for a long time we have attached to them some other thing...

POSTILLION: Calm down a little, you're all sweaty...

STADELMANN: [*wiping his forehead*] Yes, it's cold, and hot too... sure that time I wasn't sweating, thirty more years are something, as far as... what month was it when we traveled around the Rhine and the Neckar? July, I think, now I understand... or was it May? No, no, May was the next year, anyway I always stayed up here...

POSTILLION: Aren't you sick yet of all this air?

STADELMANN: [*not listening*] The rocks we gathered, and all those other strange things—And those wines in Markobrunn, in Hattenheim, God bless them, they tasted like flowers, like like... we did all the inns, one by one... and even if I got a little carried away, you can't forget that sometimes even he—[*turning to the postillion*] When we walked into a tavern I would head straight for the kitchen, they all came out, the host and hostess and the girls who washed dishes, everybody celebrating, shouting: "Carl, Carl! Carl's here!"

VOICE FROM INSIDE THE COACH: So what's going on up there, Stadelmann, that you are shrieking like an eagle?

STADELMANN: Yes, of course, I've almost forgotten that I'm called Carl, now everybody calls me Stadelmann…

POSTILLION: A lousy life, huh, being the butler to a gentleman like that, who probably wanted to be waited on hand and foot…

STADELMANN: Well what do you think, I even wrote his diary for him, you bet, I wasn't only good for copying…it seems like they want to publish it, you know? Sometimes the Counselor scolded me, when I read him what I had written about the peasants' misery and the luxury of those dumb, lazy country squires…the world is round, Stadelmann, he used to say, it's useless trying to make it square…but deep, deep down he didn't think that way either.

POSTILLION: Well, you try to understand these gentlemen of ours…When they want to start acting like us—just for a little while, you know, then they get tired of it, yet…

STADELMANN: [*looking into the distance*] How blue everything looks from far away! When we're down there too, it's not that we will be inside that blue...the color of absence, he used to say, of loss, of what's missing...so, for me, of everything, of life...what nonsense, I'm really getting senile [*he drinks*] Yes, so much blue...and so little...blue...even Lori's eyes were blue, a deep blue, almost black...like her hair, so black it almost looked blue, night blue, a dark night but shining too, which made you think of faraway, hidden stars...

POSTILLION: I was getting ready to say that sooner or later a skirt would appear, you really don't look like the type that doesn't—Who was this with blue, no, dark eyes, anyway...

STADELMANN: She was someone truly fascinated by minerals, you know, rocks, and she would study them...you should have seen her when she smiled, she tilted her head a little towards her shoulder and shut those dark eyes, obliquely lowering her brows on two somewhat prominent cheeks, but just a little, little bit like those Hungarian ladies you see at the Karlsbad spa, in those places there...yes, she looked at you like that, sideways, as if she was tired, and so tender, in that tiredness...myopic eyes always seem full of sweetness, the counselor used to say, in this way a beautiful woman who is a little myopic is often so enchanting...He was the one who protected her, because he taught her, guided her a little in mineralogy, you understand, given that she was so passionate, as he said, but then...

Lights go out; when they come back up shortly, we still see the outline of the coach. A few yards ahead, Stadelmann—a lot younger—and Lori are busy collecting rocks.

STADELMANN: There, he will certainly like this one, see how white and shiny it is.

LORI: [*she is a young woman, she takes the rock in hand*] How smooth and polished it is—

STADELMANN: It must have been in the water a long time, who knows how it got all the way here. Water is what polishes things, makes them so shiny, so sweet and round. Once, on the Main—

LORI: Did he teach you, this passion for minerals?

STADELMANN: Well...in a certain sense, yes, even if—certainly without him I would have never, as you say, applied myself...but even I, for my part...remember the tourmaline we saw yesterday in the display case?

LORI: The one that one minute looked dark red and the next light blue, and then sometimes transparent? Simply beautiful—

STADELMANN: [*coming up to her and looking into*

her eyes] Yes, blue and very beautiful, like your eyes… [*adopting a different tone*] You know it's a silicate, right? *Lapis electricus,* it's called, because it's drawn to other bodies…do you like dancing?

LORI: ~~Now what does dancing have to do with any-~~ thing…

STADELMANN: [*with a haughty air*] Nothing, though if we want, it could have everything to do with it, of course. All we'd have to do is go to the White Stag tonight…

LORI: Please, you know that tonight is the reception [*she sits*].

STADELMANN: [*sitting next to her*] I know, there's always something, you can do everything but get on with living…even as a child the hardest thing was playing with the dog…the field was behind the house, the dog always there, there wasn't anything in the world I liked better. But when I'd begin running after him, there was always something: Carl, come here! Carl, go get some wood, Carl, come and say goodbye to the professor…so I would go back, the dog stayed there a while watching me and then he'd take off running again, by himself.

LORI: You know how to tell a story so well, Stadelmann.

STADELMANN: Just for you, I don't feel like telling
others a thing, just some bragging…this, for
instance, about the dog, I've never told anyone,
I didn't even remember it, it's you who made it
come to mind…you know, when you smile like
that, tilting your head and shutting your eyes a
little, there, I'd like to tell you everything, no, in
fact, I'd like to stay here and listen to you…

LORI: You are very sweet, Stadelmann.

STADELMANN: Carl…

LORI: Yes, Carl…

GOETHE'S VOICE: [*from inside the coach*] Stadelmann,
please ask the young lady to come back inside the
carriage, we are going on to the chateau, in the
meantime see to those bottles of Hochheimer
which you ordered in Kräuter, mind you, there
are only three left.

*Lori gets up and moves towards the carriage;
Stadelmann gets up too, following her with his eyes.
Lights go out and come up again on the previous
scene with Stadelmann up on the box, next to the
postillion.*

STADELMANN: Just like with the dog, the same thing

... those eyes, those somewhat irregular features, that black hair falling over her shoulder when she tilted her head and timidly laughed ... I could have passed my whole life watching her ... instead, everybody always shouting: Carl here, Stadelmann there ...

POSTILLION: Well, we're lacking everything but certainly not pains in the ass.

STADELMANN: [*rousing himself*] So, now they've gone to the other world, all of them, and I'm still up here, alive, and on my way to Frankfurt ... Onward, faster, faster! [*he gets excited, as if he's spurring on the horses*] The doctor is coming, make way for the doctor, my hat is the doctor straight from the University of Jena!

SCENE 2

In an inn, during a stopover on his trip. Stadelmann is at table, a little tipsy, holding forth with the innkeeper and other locals.

STADELMANN: [*shouting, with grand gestures*] No sir, don't even think it, the students are totally entitled to have parties and dances to their heart's content, nothing wrong there, in fact, every occasion is the right one to have some beautiful girls within reach, first a few sweet words, then you sing, you dance, then you reach out your hands and the rest takes care of itself—but without all this clowning around with politics and revolution, and all this talk in the air from hot and empty heads, which finally even ruin the party! That students should think about studying and screwing, to each his own! [*he guzzles his drink and fills his glass again*]

INNKEEPER: Exactly right, so that at least they won't get the rest of us in trouble, because every time they start singing that gibberish about revolution and liberty, the next day the cops are in here bothering us, and maybe even closing us down!

POSTILLION: [*drinking*] Sure, it's always us, the ones who get screwed! Of course, I myself—

YOUNG MAN: Shame on you, with people like you we will always be slaves—wake up, Germany!

ANOTHER: Yes, long live Germany! [*they start singing the Rhine Song*] O stranger, we'll never settle for less/ than the free German Rhineland…

STADELMANN: Clowns, Germany doesn't mean a thing, it's a trap for fanatics!

A MAN: [*evidently someone traveling with Stadelmann*] Calm down, Stadelmann.

POSTILLION: Yes, it isn't something to get so upset over. Of course, I myself—

STADELMANN: A true German looks to Europe and the world, remember what Goethe told us!

THE FIRST YOUNG MAN: He was somebody who kissed Napoleon's and the princes' feet, and you were the one who licked his!

STADELMANN: And you can kiss my ass, fool!

YOUNG MAN: It's just because you're old with one foot in the grave, or else—

STADELMANN: Try it, boy, and I'll show you [*he gets up and starts towards him; the others jump in between, and calm is somewhat restored*]

THE MAN FROM BEFORE: Now, Stadelmann, I implore you—

ANOTHER CUSTOMER: [*to Stadelmann*] You've become too used to palaces, you, even though you might sleep in the attic…the peasants that rot in the barns work themselves to death and die of hunger, while the gentry scratch themselves all day and stuff themselves like pigs!

STADELMANN: You're telling me, traveling with the Counselor I used to write down in his diary all the crap done to the poor that I saw going on around me? We know that the cause of revolution lies with the fucking gentry, but when the revolution is unleashed and the mob rages, it's just other fucking bosses that start chopping heads to fatten their sausages with blood, the way you do with pigs when making blood sausages…only a just ruler and order can stand in the way of anarchy and injustice…and…and…and anyway…

CUSTOMER: The world has changed, my friend, and not even a Goethe could do anything…don't get so worked up over those songs and those duels and those beer drunks of the students, I'm not happy about them either, but that isn't the point…

STADELMANN: Right, but just the fact that they like beer so much already starts getting to me.

CUSTOMER: Beer or wine…but have you looked around, did you see how many people there are, people who are needy, who change, who can't keep pulling the load as before, as always—maybe from your window you can't see them, these faces that still yawn stunned, but they are beginning to look around…it's going to take more than a good prince who offers you a drink on your birthday, my friend—

YOUNG MAN: It is the prince who makes unjust laws, and the law that makes injustice!

ANOTHER: We must rebel, show them something!

STADELMANN: But to whom, stupid? We have to act

justly, with patience, with…with…what was I saying, I've lost my thought…[*he drinks*] yes, I was saying that with order there is culture, and…and culture teaches respect and thus not to do people harm…and…and anyway if you first ~~sweep in front of your own door, meanwhile~~—[*he accidentally knocks over a bottle and a plate, which end up on the floor*]

YOUNG MAN: You start picking up this crap!

POSTILLION: Why are you all getting so heated up? Of course, I myself—

ANOTHER YOUNG MAN: You are an insult to true Germans!

STADELMANN: I don't give a damn about true Germans…Humanity, yes, humanity…

ANOTHER: Long live Germany, long live liberty!

ANOTHER: War on the palaces, peace for the barns!

STADELMANN: Germans will never be a people! Goethe—

ONE OF THE YOUNG MEN: [*he slaps him*] Here's one for you, renegade, rogue, and for your master too!

STADELMANN: [*he jumps on him, stumbles, falls on the floor pulling down plates and bottles after him*] Cowards, lousy animals, wait till—

INNKEEPER: Enough, go call somebody, they're going to smash everything! [*The postilion and the other traveler help Staldelmann to his feet and push him towards the door*]

MAN: Let's go, we're leaving. Aren't you ashamed, at your age... [*They exit*]

SCENE 3

Frankfurt, in front of the Hotel Swan. It is night, Stadelmann has just arrived and he is saying goodbye to those on the coach, about to leave.

POSTILLION: Great, I'm glad they have put you up well. Yes, yes, very well. Now I'm going to drive this heap to the post office, and I'll be done with today too. Well, goodnight [*he moves into the background, where we see the outline of the coach, and exits*]

STADELMANN: [*at the hotel entrance*] Goodnight... [*he takes a few steps in the street*] What a strange moon... the sky is clear but with this light things seem veiled, hidden... who knows what things, but then... that down there, with the two low towers, must be the church of St. Leonard... all dark, even this time... we were never done wandering around, that night... well, you know, it must have been July, or August, the air was warm—and he, how he held onto my arm, with that swollen foot, it was me doing the walking for the two of us... how strong you are, Stadelmann, he told me when we came around the corner of the square ...and when we finally were in front of his house, there on the Hirschgraben, where he was born, everything shut down in that quiet, I felt for an instant his arm had no strength, he was giving up and leaning on me like a child, almost letting himself go... and when an old clock, inside the house, started striking the hour, and I said to him, like that, just to be saying something, "like once upon a time, Excellency, when you were a child, who knows how moving it must be to think about the past," he pulled away from me and he says, very hard and formal, "the past doesn't exist, Stadelmann, it is late, let's go to sleep," and off he went alone, dragging that swollen foot behind, standing up straight and rather quick...

He has wandered a bit down the street, talking to himself. From the corner a female figure comes up to him, like a shadow.

SHADOW: Half a thaler, sweetheart, an hour for a thaler...

STADELMANN: And after ten minutes, what would we
    do for the rest of the time? I know I look good
    for my age, but over sixty—

THE SHADOW: You could explain minerals to me, show
    me the tourmaline...

STADELMANN: What? Who are you? I must be crazy,
    or drunk—

SHADOW: [*stepping back*] Step up, get in the carriage,
    not like that time—

STADELMANN: What stupid tricks...

SHADOW: The night is dark, blue, like black black hair,
    and even shiny...

STADELMANN: Enough... I'd rather pay a thaler, even
    for nothing...

SHADOW: You mean to say just for a smile, a smile
    like this...

STADELMANN: It can't be, I'm not—wait, please, come
    here—

SHADOW: Why didn't you love me? It was so easy, to
    be happy... [*she disappears*]

STADELMANN: Yes, I loved you, yes... but it wasn't easy,
    everything was so difficult... [*stretches out his
    arms*] Where are you, where have you gone...

SCENE 4

Frankfurt, a large room in the Römer, the City Hall, in which they are preparing the Goethe celebration. Numerous people, surrounding Stadelmann.

STADELMANN: A ducat, I put a ducat in their pocket, those from the theater's orchestra, so that they might play a beautiful serenade at dawn, for his birthday, the 28th of August of...of...yes, of 1815, they were, you know, his happy days with Marianne Willemer, when they were interested in Persian poetry...anyway, a whole ducat, and then doesn't that guy go ruin everything with—

A WOMAN: And the wife of that shoemaker in Erfurt?

STADELMANN: Ah, Mrs. Vogel, a beauty, a real beauty, plump and round...well, he wanted to be sure because, he always liked the houris from the Moslem paradise, as he called them...A woman must be a moon, a full moon...But above all, as he kept repeating at Erfurt in front of those poppy fields, they shouldn't be spoilsports—

A CITY COUNCILMAN: Which poets did he like best?

STADELMANN: Sure, he liked many, too many, kind and indulgent as he was…but a poet, the only truly great poet was him, and I know more than little about this…

ECCLESIASTICAL ADVISOR: Even if in his own peculiar way, he was a great and devoted religious spirit…

STADELMANN: Certainly, more than all the priests in the world. That sense of his, how should I say…yes, of the divine, of everything, of each thing…

HIGH SCHOOL PROFESSOR: And his unapproachable art, so Greek, so German, so edifying for our youth…for me, his masterpiece remains *Herman and Dorothy,* with his ethics that surpass the revolution's tempest…

STADELMANN: His masterpiece, he used to say, was his *Theory of Colors,* and he would've known what he was talking about, right? I, in my modest way, contributed to that immortal work—

A WOMAN: Is it true, apropos, that he considered himself immortal?

STADELMANN: [*uncertain*] Are you asking if, as a old man, he wasn't thinking he should die? Well, there, it's true that at a certain age one…however…

ECCLESIASTICAL ADVISOR: Those pronouncements of his, his extremely lofty air, always so even-tempered, so wise—

STADELMANN: Yes, but he was also a character, you go figure him...like that time he ordered me to put a bottle of wine, red wine, in a window, with a glass, and another, with another glass, in the other window. And he began going back and forth in the room, first to one window, downing a glass, then to the other, downing another glass, and so on, back and forth, until he asked me: it's the twenty-eighth, yes? And I, no, Excellency, it's the twenty-seventh. Idiot, he said, you think you know more than me? It's the twenty-eighth, my birthday. Beg your pardon, Excellency, I say, but today is the twenty-seventh. Give me the calendar, animal, and I took it to him, he looked at it and exclaimed, holy cow, you're right, it is the twenty-seventh, and I got drunk for nothing! [*All laugh*]

ONE OF THOSE PRESENT: How was he, Goethe, really?

STADELMANN: Him? Well...how to say...grand, it's the only word, truly grand. When he would put on his table the *Trilogy of Passion,* in blue bindings, and he told me to light two candles, and he would start reading out loud those verses which I too am in, yes, he even put me in there, one of those "faithful comrades" is me, actually me…when I listened I felt that in there was everything, happiness, sorrow, farewell, all those things we never had, and maybe not even he…

PROFESSOR: I don't understand…

STADELMANN: Nor do I, there's little to understand…

A FUNCTIONARY: [*showing him a Goethe death mask*] This we will put in the vestibule, right after the entrance, so that visitors, just entering…you remembered him younger, didn't you? Yes, because in the last eight years, after—

STADELMANN: Go ahead, spit it out, after he fired me…But what does eight years more or less matter, a mask is a mask, they're all the same, taken at thirty, at fifty, at ninety…sure, because it's always the mask of a dead man, and the dead have no age…look at this face all nicely rested and satisfied, with the air of someone who says, there were things to be done I did them and now everything is fine. Instead, nothing is fine, when you are dead…

A WOMAN: Anyway, don't you find quite a resemblance?

STADELMANN: [*holding up the mask*] Do you really think a face like this could write *Werther* or *Faust*? Look [*he pinches his flabby cheeks and chin, he tugs at the skin under his eyes*] don't you see this empty and moldy flab, these bags under my eyes, do you think that he didn't have them, he that at certain times even had a ridiculous belly, and those crooked legs? It's exactly because—

A COUNCILMAN: Please, Mr. Stadelmann, this is not the time—

A VOICE IN THE GROUP: What a peasant, I told you so…

ECCLESIASTICAL ADVISOR: Well, the weakness of the flesh, of course, it is a noble sentiment, but…

STADELMANN: [*going on*] It's exactly because he knew it, knew to the bottom of his heart what misery and stink is this carcass of ours and what bad breath comes out after a serious bout of drinking, that he was a great poet, the single, greatest poet…this nice, refined and silly mask, indeed, good enough for any half-assed…

A COUNCILMAN: [*coughing*] Fine, fine…now let's move on to the other room, you will see how interesting…[*he moves, with Stadelmann and the others, to the adjoining room*] Here we see his shells, the pieces of lava and some of the famous drawings of the jaw bone, his great discovery…

A WOMAN: They say the idea came to him examining the head of a sheep found in the sand.

ANOTHER WOMAN: Yes, yes, that in fact at first he had mistaken it for the head of a Jew.

A PATRICIAN: It would have been a billy-goat, then—

STADELMANN: Always a lot better than so many of the airheads you see around… he would get furious, the Counsellor, when he heard somebody going on about the Jews—hear that, he used to say, do you hear that ass who wants to have his say against Spinoza…

THE PREVIOUS COUNCILMAN: [*trying to get past the moment's embarrassment*] Please, notice the human jawbone and compare it with that, on table II, of a babirusa, or, even better, with that, on table IV, of a walrus, of a very young walrus, as the poet expressly described.

A WOMAN: How long do they live, walruses?

COUNCILMAN: This is a cast of a mammoth tusk, look what a tusk, and what a beautiful color, truly faithful to the original.

PATRICIAN: It's enormous and when you think it's only one tooth…

PROFESSOR: It's monstrous…

STADELMANN: Sure, I didn't even remember it being that big... yet it was I who took that cast and colored it as he wanted, and took it to Count Sternberg to see... he had a real passion for this thing, there was no end to talking about it, he and the Count—

ECCLESIASTICAL ADVISOR: What did he find to be so interesting?

STADELMANN: What... it's clear, isn't it? My God, clear... maybe one feels like he's growing old, they tell him he's written immortal works and he understands that and then he sees this thing that's so huge and thinks it was in the mouth of this animal centuries ago, no millennia, thousands and thousands of years ago, anyway I don't know how many, it doesn't matter, and then...

ECCLESIASTICAL ADVISOR: You certainly knew him quite well, Stadelmann, we can see you were very close to him, I am delighted.

STADELMANN: [*flattered*] Anyway...

A WOMAN: How does a poet become interested in these dry things, all these bones and these skeletons...

STADELMANN: [*seriously*] He was interested in the grand laws of nature, madam, which, as he used to say, if it gave one an advantage it always made one vulnerable, so it all comes around... [*looking a little bewildered at the tusk*] Who knows where this huge beast was vulnerable, that with a tusk like this—and yet it must have had some defect, in fact it's no longer around, it's extinct...

PROFESSOR: Yes, the classic state means equilibrium, in nature as with man, and the great poet—

STADELMANN: [*almost an aside*] ...but then for every flaw there ought to be a benefit and an old man, for instance, a little by little loses strength and health on one hand, he ought to acquire who knows what thing on the other, and instead... who knows what it heard, this old beast, when it went around with those huge drooping ears... yes, I think that the Counsellor, even if he really thought himself more important than the half-wits all around him [*he unintentionally glances around*] and it made him see too, think once in a while that this forgotten beast might be greater than him, I don't know if you understand—

PROFESSOR: Yes, of course, the poet meditates upon the frailty of man and upon nature... and it must have been painful for him, with his sensibility—

STADELMAN: What pain, he had a hide like an elephant's, the mammoth's, indeed, the whole world was for him a fly that he, bang, would waste no time squashing and brushing away—today's poet, indeed, these disasters, this kind of little beggar, as he called them, only capable of suffering, if not, they're afraid of not being poets... While for him it mattered above all that nothing, not even poetry, would ruin the party...how I hate them too, all these spoilsports, even if... [*the festive noises and chatter grow louder, some waiters enter with some trays with cups of wine, pleasant music in the background, and Stadelmann looks around*]...even if I don't know which party, neither here nor there, either now or before, there is to ruin...

SCENE 5

It is night. Stadelmann is in his lodgings, near a window covered with ice.

STADELMANN: [*he runs his finger over the glass*] What did he used to say? Ah, that's it...if you clean with your finger glass fogged over with your breath and right away blow on it again [*blows on the glass*] for a few moments you see fluctuating, mixed-up and bright colors...it's true, there...but how quick they disappear... [*he drinks*] it must be really cold outside, everything's iced over... what strange shapes ice makes, flowers, crystals, frills... it looks like a faraway landscape, this here might be a lake [*he points his finger on the glass*], and these the trees, and there a mountain... [*he moves back a little staring at the glass*] and what's that there, who is that ugly mug, that broken-down, nasty face... yes, that's me [*touching the glass with his finger*] it's my reflection in the glass, but who's that other one back there, drawn by the cold, with those icy eyebrows, and that crooked mouth...? why are you looking at me and making those faces, who do you think you are, the devil? [*laughs and drinks*] Go on, if it wasn't for this cold you couldn't even be here, without those icicles you wouldn't even have a face—[*pulls his head back a little and looks*] how strange though seeing those two faces, mine... and that other...

Well, there's no two without three, how much does it take to make a third [*blows on the glass, fogging it, and draws a face with his finger*] There! Now all three of you go screw yourselves, for me it's all the same! [*he grimaces at the glass, every once in a while tossing down a mouthful of drink*]

85

Enough now, get lost! [*he erases his side of the glass and he bangs above it to make the ice on the outside fall*]

Look, look, it seems like a snow storm, a dance, a torchlight procession [*he raises the candelabra and watches the fine spray of icicles that fall glistening in the light's reflection, the bright drops that slip down the glass*]

What stars, pearls, necklaces...and those stripes, those scribbles on the glass, like illegible writing...like that inscription in the old, abandoned synagogue, of which he told me to take a cast and then he looked over those complicated marks, without understanding anything, as now I don't understand a thing...maybe it's a message from that ugly face from before, and so much the better for who can't read it...

[*runs his finger over the glass and then blows on the glass*] There are the colors again, and now they disappear, the last to disappear, as he used to say, is blue...

SCENE 6

In the Schlosser house, the nephews of Goethe's brother-in-law. They are throwing a party for Stadelmann, who telling in a lively and joking manner his adventures in those days.

A MAID [*rather old*]: Ah, Carl, you are always the same! When you first suddenly walked in the back door, you gave me quite a start…

STADELMANN: [*putting his arms around her*] Yes, women are always afraid, but then—

MAID: [*pushing him away laughing*] Be good—

COOK: How did it go at City Hall?

STADELMANN: A real, proper coronation, like in the old days! [*he sits in an armchair*] We, Sacred Roman Emperor of the Poorhouse of Jena [*laughter, he drinks from a bottle on the table*] Servants, a nice bow, if not—[*he picks up a broom and threatens them*] With this scepter—

A WAITER: And the women?

STADELMANN: The noblest and most beautiful, I can't tell you what a pick-me-up! Then those fans [*picks up a rag and imitates the ladies' fanning*] those bows, that hand-kissing [*takes the hands of*

*the maid and the cook and kisses them with exag-
gerated respect*] And those lackeys at City Hall,
always with their backs bent like marionettes... [*he
makes mechanical and repeated bows*]

Schlosser enters, the owner of the house.

SCHLOSSER: Dear Stadelmann—

STADELMANN: [*composing himself*] Good evening, Mr.
Schlosser, I came by to give my regards. I thought
I would see you at City Hall, but—

SCHLOSSER: [*coolly*] No, we weren't there.

STADELMANN: [*a little tipsy*] Well, at bottom the poet's
true family is a spiritual one... [*reciting*] Is it for
nothing, woman, that what there is between us
is written?

COOK: Nothing, luckily.

STADELMANN: [*to Schlosser*] Be sure that the family, if
modestly, was well-represented. I spoke, explained,
told stories...

SCHLOSSER: Yes, fine, fine. Goodbye, Stadelmann,
good luck [*exits*].

STADELMANN: Goodbye... [*he grows quiet*]

MAID: What's wrong now, cat got your tongue?

STADELMANN: [*shaking himself*] Yes, when that two-bit
professor wanted to explain to me, to me, Goethe's
poetry, I showed him, plain and simple the how

and why … [*his voice lapses into chattering, as the lights dim and go out*].

SCENE 7

A dining room in a private home, richly appointed. At table the burgomaster, the city's bigwigs, ladies, patricians, rich burghers, literary people. From a window we se, at the end of a square, Goethe's monument, inaugurated a short time before. Stadelmann is seated next to the burgomaster—who is standing and just finishing a speech—in front of a window out of which we see the monument. He is well-groomed, with the shoes he was given at the poorhouse and Goethe's old coat and tails.

BURGOMASTER: … of a poetry, I was saying, of a universal poetry that lifts the soul to higher things! I am certain that the poet's spirit will forgive me if I dare say that here, in this moment of profound joy, even his troubled hero, even Faust, would have surely said, as each one of us: a moment, wait, you are beautiful! [*everyone applauds, he lifts his glass, mimicked by the rest*]

Allow me now to lift a glass for our guest, a

humble and loyal man who had the privilege
to be near the great poet, to live for years, each
day, in his shadow, I say, in his light, our good
Stadelmann!

VOICES: Long live Stadelmann!

STADELMANN: [*he is quite moved and we see he has
been drinking, but he is composed and dignified*]
Thank you, ladies and gentlemen, thank you.

A VOICE: A toast, Stadelmann, a speech!

STADELMANN: Me, a speech? No, no—

BURGOMASTER: Courage, Mr. Stadelmann, you are
among friends! And then, look down there, doesn't
it seem that even he is telling you to speak, you
wouldn't want to disobey him—

STADELMANN: [*he gets up a little shaky*] How can I,
after so much kindness, even if truly…
[*taking glass in hand, in a jaunty tone*] To
him, then [*vaguely pointing, with glass in hand,
toward the monument we see beyond the window*]
I never said no, he didn't even need to tell me
something that I had already understood and
satisfied him…

BURGOMASTER: Bravo, Stadelmann, bravo, you were
truly a loyal servant.

STADELMANN: Of course before, when they pulled

down the sheet and I saw him so solemn, calm and undisturbed, it wasn't that . . . well, sure, you know, he's made of stone, he certainly can't get excited, but—[*stifled giggles all around*]

BURGOMASTER: Ladies and gentlemen, please! So then, Stadelmann—

STADELMANN: Yet he, he was never one to get excited, even when he was alive . . . truly a beautiful statue, congratulations . . . although that face, those empty eyes . . . The Counselor's were chestnut, brown, with a blue circle around the iris that sometimes appeared light gray, and when he looked at you—and that face there now . . . I know that a face doesn't mean anything, you put it on like a hat, and even us, here, it's not that—[*he looks around, someone laughs, someone claps, we hear some someone else mumbling:* "it's fine to have a good time, but if he wants to be rude . . . I told you so, this wasn't the right thing . . ."]

BURGOMASTER: Well, Stadelmann . . .

STADELMANN: And that mantel, with all those buttons—look instead at his coat and tails, his real one, the one he gave me—[*he puts down the glass and shows everyone the coat and tails, fingering the lapel*]

See this? Here, right here, there was his Legion of honor, and here next to it the Order of St. Anne, yes, the one from the Czar, and a little lower the Austrian, the Order of Leopold... now you see only a couple of stains, yet—

BURGOMASTER: Good, bravo... [*in solemn tone*] My dear Mr. Stadelmann, this noble city, which was the birthplace of the greatest German poet, wants to offer you a small, tangible souvenir of this unforgettable day! [*he holds out a small pouch of money, which Stadelmann takes and holds for a few confused moments in his hand, mumbling* "thank you, thank you..." *and then putting it in his pocket. Applause, cheer* "Long live Stadelmann!"] In addition the city of Frankfurt has decided to assign you a small annual pension, which will be available to you at Jena through the auspices of the poorhouse, until you are able to make more decorous arrangements, as for the rest—[*stopping himself embarrassed*]

STADELMANN: Yes, as for the rest...

BURGOMASTER: And now—

STADELMANN: Yes, right away... thank you, I thank you, I am moved, pardon me... how the glasses shine, and the candelabras, and the wine... gold, silver and ruby, yellow, white and red…always colors, how they glisten, and dazzle…no I—[*he swigs, puts the glass down and leans on the table*]

BURGOMASTER: Good, to your health, Stadelmann, and then—[*lifts his glass*]

STADELMANN: [*lifting his glass too*] Cheers! There, I…what can I say? I wish you…You know what he used to say, when anybody came around who wanted to hear his wise, immortal words? They were continually coming and going, they never left us in peace, we couldn't take it anymore…He sat there silently in front of a bottle of red wine and you had to wait, everybody quiet, until he was through thinking, until he, after having thought, would get up and say: "Gentlemen, I wish you good night!"

[*Laughter, some clapping,* "so anyway"]

A WOMAN: He would say that even if his visitor were a beautiful lady?

STADELMANN: [*lifting his glass*] Good night, goodnight to you all! Gentlemen and beautiful ladies, the falling night makes no distinctions, if there's peace on every hill and dale…peace and silence, as the rocks teach us, these old teachers from whom we have a lot to learn, and most of all to learn that we have nothing to say, like them... 'Don't tell anyone, only the wisest men, because people will only jeer'... [*others mumbling*] Sure, you only need to be him, to write poems, and also to be quiet—And I [*puts down his glass and looks around confused, almost stunned, as we hear amused and irritated comments, then he pulls himself together and raises another glass*]

Cheers! Do you see how the light reflects in the glass and the wine? I want to tell you one more story, a good story, truly good... once I picked up a glass of wine, white wine, then I put it under a sheet of paper, that was white too—[*he gestures with his goblet and a napkin, trying awkwardly to give an idea of the experiment*] there, like this—and as you see, no, standing there, you can't see anything, you all ought to stand on this side, well, anyway—here the light passes through the wine—watch, Excellency, I tell him, if we turn the glass like this [*he turns it*] there is one sun, if we turn it like this, there are two and instead like this, *voilà*, there are three, three suns, and we also see the rainbow, look, just as in the sky... and he, you know, you know what he said? "You are a genius, Stadelmann!"

[*he pauses: for an instant, on the wall, Goethe's*

silhouette appears and we hear his voice: "You are a genius, Stadelmann!"]

VOICES: Bravo! But how do you do it, you have to turn the glass? Well, what do you know! But of course, it might be…bravo!

STADELMANN: Yes, he actually said that…and he added that I was more economical than nature, because for me one glass of wine was enough to make everything appear…yet, wine was always enough for me, only with that was I able to do anything…You ought to see what marvelous suns and what a rainbow in here [*he raises his glass, turns it, studies it*] How many suns, how many rainbows and it all shines, quivers and vanishes…yes, a toast, I'll drink just one [*drinks*], then another and yet another and even the rainbow, a sip for every color, no, a bottle, seven bottles, seven times seven—[*he knocks over the glass on the tablecloth and trying to straighten up knocks another over, as those nearest him draw away*] Sorry, I'm very sorry…

BURGOMASTER: It's nothing, nothing…but now we must really be going [*signals a waiter*] Please see Mr. Stadelmann to the Swan

[*The waiter draws near Stadelmann and takes him by the arm*]

STADELMANN: Thank you, sorry... You are a genius,
Stadelmann... amusing, yes? A genius...

*He moves towards the exit with the waiter, as the lights
dim. Curtain.*

ACT III

SCENE 1

Jena. Stadelmann is in his bed at the poorhouse, and he is tossing and turning between sleep and drowsiness.

STADELMANN: 'Well, leave me, loyal comrades, to endure it... But you, the world's before you. On. Explore it, the whole wide earth'... let them go on and laugh about the ridiculous old man, but I'd like to see them write verses like this... blue, Ulrike's too were blue, but you have to know how to get away, cut all ties, off and away in a carriage, away from everything, even from her and from yourself... Away, away, much quicker, before they notice that I've dirtied the tablecloth, that the superintendent asks me to show him the bill, the soap list—what's there to look at under the table, I know that the soles are worn out and the pants are all ragged, there at the bottom, I have already, in writing, brought this to the attention of the library's most revered secretary that it is certainly not proper even for His Excellency that I go about like this, and in fact for His Excellency's celebration, who knows what the neighbors, envious as they are, will say to his mother, poor Madam Aja, it's been years she has been waiting for a visit after all he is her son and he ought to be able to find time, what does it matter that she is dead, it's not a good excuse, certainly even I, always going here and there, don't get a chance to see my wife, yet, separating is death, she used to say...slower, much slower, why hurry to arrive in that rat hole, even if now I want to see...what, Steffi? ah, I'm a genius, you say it too, yes squeeze me, what a big, white throat, you still have those freckles on your breast, the moon, two moons, hold me, not like this, you're suffocating me, you're pulling me down, you're making me spill my glass... [*he quickly awakens and looks around, sitting up in bed, while the others are snoring*]

CUSTODIAN: [*enters for wake-up call*] Get moving, off those mattresses.

STADELMANN: [*still sitting on his bed, an aside*] Right, way over there is already a thin strip of blue, a thin strip of blue light...separating is death...he is dead, who knows where she is and I'm here...yes, here— [*the old men wake up and get out of bed*]

CUSTODIAN: [*to Stadelmann*] You too, hurry up.

STADELMANN: [*gets up*] I'm coming, I'm coming...a
    few days, and then—
CUSTODIAN: Yeah, we know, then they're coming for
    you with white horses—let's go, let's go.
AN OLD MAN: Is it true they're going to give you a
    pension?
ANOTHER, TO HIS NEIGHBOR: What pension, it's all
    made up, to give himself airs!
ANOTHER: Ah, so they're giving him a pension, so he
    can slip away? Sure, when you're born lucky...

They head for the door, Stadelmann along with them.

SCENE 2

*A dormitory in the poorhouse, in which the other old
men are waiting for Stadelmann. He is at the door, just
finishing talking to Amalia Schoppe, the actress.*

STADELMANN:...see? It's written just like that, on the
    dinner invitation [*he shows her a card*], "Mon-
    sieur Stadelmann." They were all speaking like
    that, Monsieur, Mister. Ah, what days...you
    know, I thought you might ask how it went and
    I took notes on everything [*pulls a notebook from*

his pocket] A little diary, just like once upon a time—

AMALIA SCHOPPE: I am really happy for you, Stadelmann... Mr. Stadelmann... it must have been wonderful. You did well to keep a diary, things become real when they are put down on paper, and you know better than I how much the poet wanted to record everything, to keep report on life.

STADELMANN: Yes, that was a fixed idea of his which he managed to stick in my head too, even if I, a diary, I only kept one when he was around, the things that happened to him... as for the things that happened to me, I wouldn't know how to put down half a sentence... and even now, finally—

AMELIA SCHOPPE: It's wonderful, it's quite wonderful to live like this, for someone greater than us... but now I must say goodbye, farewell. And I'm sure, as we were saying earlier, that you will be careful not to...

STADELMANN: Certainly, certainly... thank you, farewell [*as she is leaving, he enters the hall where they welcome him and greet him as if at a party*]

VOICES: Long live, Carl, welcome back! [*someone yells* "Here is Goethe," *answered by the others shutting him up with* "what a cabbage head, moron!"]

STADELMANN: Oh my…thanks, friends, I didn't know, I didn't think…

AN OLD MAN: Here, we thought that maybe you'd like this, look how lovely [*he hands him a pipe*]

STADELMANN: [*turning it between his fingers*] Thank you, truly lovely…

ANOTHER OLD MAN: Now at least you can't suck on anything better.

A THIRD OLD MAN: Would you show us how many thalers they gave you?

STADELMANN: [*pulling them out of his pocket*] Here, these are the last.

FIRST OLD MAN: Is it really true that they've given you a pension?

STADELMANN: Yes, yes…

ANOTHER OLD MAN: So you can leave this dump?

ANOTHER: Speaking of which, my shoes?

STADELMANN: Yes, the shoes, I must give them back, certainly—

FIRST OLD MAN: Go on, tells us something, how was the reception, the ceremony, the party…

ANOTHER: It must have been quite moving…once even I—

OTHER VOICES: Go on, Carl, tell us!

STADELMANN: Ah, it was all splendid, splendid…anyway the hotel, you should've seen...and then they were all so kind, majestic...lovely, lovely, yes, but in any case, the effect...

AN OLD MAN: And the dinner, what did they serve?

STADELMANN: Every blessed thing, trout, roast rabbit, goose liver, white and red wines...and lots of people, candelabras, magnificent vases...and then the speeches, and all of them asking me...

AN OLD MAN: And you?

STADELMANN: I gave them the whole song and dance, even about that time he made a mistake about his birthday, when he thought it was the twenty-eighth and instead it was the twenty-seventh...

AN OLD MAN: As far as that goes, you don't need to be Goethe, even Franz here, the last few months when he was out of it, he always thought it was Monday.

ANOTHER: So anyhow, what was there special?

STADELMANN: Many, so many things! I don't know, for instance...look, you had to have been there, if not, telling it like this...the square at night, completely dark and with ice on the windows...

AN OLD MAN: Sure, because here instead it's hot and the sun shines at night.

STADELMANN: Anyway, I assure you...I've always known how to tell stories well about things, things

that were happening...and now like this, on my
own two feet, not—maybe there is nothing to tell,
nothing happened...

   [*Disappointed murmurs, disapproval, embarrassment*]

AN OLD MAN: What did I tell you...

SCHRAMEK: Well, let's have a drop. [*he drinks*]

STADELMANN: So many grand portraits on the walls,
   nothing like these blank walls...

AN OLD MAN: At least you did some good eating,
   lucky you.

STADELMANN: Anyway, thank you...thank you
   [*drinks*]

SCENE 3

*In the poorhouse dormitory. Stadelmann is alone putting
away some things, pulling them out of a big travel bag.*

STADELMANN: The pants I've already given back,
   here are the shoes, and then everything's taken
   care of, there's nothing left to take care of. How
   much heavier, this bag, when I left it seemed I
   had taken a lot of stuff, and now—Ah, the coat
   and tails—but where did the medals go, you

almost can't see it anymore, with this raggedy fabric... all here, anyhow, a piece of fabric that wears out a little more on this side and a little less on the other... [*he folds the empty bag and puts it under the bed*]

SCENE 4

In the poorhouse garden. Stadelmann and Schramek working on the woodpile.

SCHRAMEK: So, will you pass me that wheelbarrow?

STADELMANN: Ah yes, sorry. [*pushing it over to him*]

SCHRAMEK: Let's hurry up with this wood, it's really cold.

    [*Stadelmann moves a log or two, distracted*]

    Not those, the others, those that still need cutting! My, if I'm the one who's got to keep his wits about him, we're in great shape.

STADELMANN: Good, Schramek, thanks...

SCHRAMEK: So, as you were saying, it was great in Frankfurt, right?

STADELMANN: Yes yes. It was even warmer.

SCHRAMEK: Ah. [*pause*] A sip?

STADELMANN: No, thanks.

SCHRAMEK: Well, I'm going inside, to put this stuff away. You pick up the sawdust and the rest, I'll leave you the broom. [*exits*]

STADELMANN: The broom... seeing it there, standing up, so distinct, with that long long handle... and yes, the broom, but then there are also the rags, the bucket, the woodshed, each thing going with the next, there's nothing at all out of place... [*he looks around and begins sweeping*]

SCENE 5

In the poorhouse garden. Stadelmann is sitting on a bench; poorly dressed, with his clothes rumpled, unshaven, hair disheveled. Near him, Steffi.

STEFFI: So now? What were you thinking about, going back to Frankfurt on foot?

STADELMANN: Oh, Steffi... I went out to take a stroll like this... you know how I like to wander around, maybe pick up a beautiful rock or two...

STEFFI: Yes, under the snow... and even on that bench,

were you looking for your rocks, snoring? If they don't find you in time, with this cold—

STADELMANN: I'd walked a fair distance, like this, without noticing…I was tired, I sat down to rest a little, and then…

STEFFI: And then you got good and drunk. Well, you can thank the flask, if you didn't catch your death, staying out there. Though you could have been a little kinder when they got there. Agreed, they really didn't have the world's best manners, but if it wasn't for them…

STADELMANN: Sure, if it wasn't for them…but who are they after all, that they can or cannot…

STEFFI: [*she sits down next to him, runs her fingers through his hair and straightens out his jacket*] Will you look at the state you're in, all rumpled—

STADELMANN: It's fine, it's fine.

STEFFI: [*taking hold of a dangling button*] You've pulled it out…maybe you were even capable of getting into a fistfight, I know you.

STADELMANN: What fistfight, be serious.

STEFFI: [*jokingly*] If you try to show up in Frankfurt like this, you'll even take those ladies by storm, so savage and wild…

STADELMANN: Please now, in Frankfurt—

STEFFI: All those famous reports you were going to make for me, this and that, when I come back I'll tell you all about it, and then we've seen who we've seen, the gentleman hasn't time anymore to come to the laundry, they made him gifts of so many shirts, all of fine silk, that he throws them away, he doesn't need to have them washed—

STADELMANN: Yes, the shirts—speaking of which, I have to return the shoes, to him there...

STEFFI: Anyway, now that you're getting a pension, who knows what a wardrobe. Let's go back inside, it's cold.

STADELMANN: Yes, yesterday—it was yesterday, right?—out there, in the countryside, it wasn't so cold...you know, there was a crow, so black in all that snowy white, really black black, and I saw her hopping here and there, every once in a while a short flight and then hopping again...and I behind, thinking, how wonderful to be able to leap like that, bang, you're on another branch, and when you don't like it anymore you're off to somewhere else, gracefully, gracefully...

STEFFI: Once upon a time you even liked a bit of flesh...but why didn't you come right away to see me? I was so eager to hear, to know—

STADELMANN: To hear what? There's not much to say.

STEFFI: For Miss Amalia you told her part and parcel...my dear, I think that lady, after all that fuss yesterday, doesn't have much use for your company.

STADELMANN: Well, that's her problem. [*he puts a hand in his pocket, looking for something*] But where—

STEFFI: Looking for your thalers? Anyway there was only one left, after all that spending yesterday, and the superintendent took charge of it, seeing that if not, he said, it too would end up in a bottle.

STADELMANN: What kind of people, ready right away to—But...

STEFFI: Have you thought about where to go, when you get your pension?

STADELMANN: Oh sure, where to go, certainly...certainly, you know, now I've got to see—

[*he stands, lifts the basket of linens*] Leave it, I'll take this inside for you... [*he moving toward the inside of the poorhouse*]

SCENE 6

In the ceiling, where the sheets are stored. Stadelmann enters from a ladder, with the basket of linens.

STADELMANN: Now, I'll put this here...no, here...well, anyway—so many sheets, washed to be once again dirtied and then dirtied to be once again washed, until finally—and yes, they unravel, they wear out, they tear...My God, if you think about how many times you get dressed and undressed in a day, for years and years...so I, let's see...twice a day...so...forty, forty-five thousand times, more or less...but where? yes, here it is, they'll never find it here, they'll never think of looking here [*he takes a bottle with a glass out from behind a laundry basket, he pours some wine, drinks, sits on a box and pours some more*]

Ah...[*tasting the wine*] Forty thousand is a fine number, it has a certain ring to it, yes, it's not for everybody, forty thousand, forty thousand...and that crow yesterday, for instance, not even one time, there's the difference, the metamorphosis of animals that interested him greatly, evolution, rising to a higher step, forty thousand steps and you arrive at humanity, to human dignity…

[*looks down at the box*] Who knows what they kept inside first…maybe apples, or potatoes—they grumble that all we get are potatoes, but with salt at least…what old wood, though still solid [*rubbing the box*]

[*empties his glass and fills it again, spilling a little on his chest*] Oh well—how quickly the fabric stains…so, another medal, a fourth, the one that was missing [*holds out his arm with glass in hand*] How the glass shines, here there's even the white paper, yes, the sheets, even out there, on the ground, it's all white, there is still just a little bit of sun, I think—

[*he gets up and stands on the box, looking toward the little window up high and holding the glass in his hand, with a scarf around the neck hanging down on his chest*]

[*looking at the scarf*] It's really almost gone, unraveled so, I need to throw it away…

Yes, there's still sun down there, over there, swollen and red like a pig's heart… [*pinkish and pulsing light reflects across the ceiling*]

But it must be in here too [*turning the glass*] there it is, and even a second, and a third, all three, and then the rainbow, like in the sky, like a snake, but why does it squeeze, it will end up shattering the glass, what's wrong with them over there that they have to open their mouths so wide, what are they thinking, even if there are three, three suns…

[*he takes off his scarf, holding it in his hand standing straight up on the box*] I'll take care of it, I'm a genius, right…and so, one down [*he drinks*], another down, and another [*he drinks*] and then even the rainbow, here, like this…[*he drinks*]

[*the lights dim, like when the sun has just gone down*]

And now white looks like gray, no, pale blue, blue…even the scarf should have had different colors, not actually seven, but—and where is it that…

He keeps talking to himself and gesticulating, standing on the box with scarf in hand.

SCENE 7

In the poorhouse dormitory. Many people, confusion.

A DOCTOR: There is nothing to be done. He was

till warm, but—[*makes a gesture of indifferent hopelessness*]

THE POORHOUSE DIRECTOR: I don't understand how this could have happened, how no one noticed—yes, someone is going to pay for this, it's the first time such a disgusting thing has happened, and yet God knows that some real wrecks have come through here—and never, I say never, in these many years...

CUSTODIAN: Look here how he carefully knotted both ropes, a real braid, and on top of that the scarf—

AN OLD MAN: What's happened?

OTHER OLD MEN: Oh God!—No, it's impossible—Who?—I saw him first, I saw his shadow up there, near the little window, dangling—Poor Carl!—But where, how...

SUPERINTENDENT: Go away, go away from there, there's already enough confusion!

AN OLD MAN: Is it true his feet were touching the ground, I mean the top of the box?

CUSTODIAN: Yes, I don't really understand how he could have hung himself, well, he must have held his feet back, like this, so— [*he gestures with his foot bent backwards*]

STEFFI: [*to the side, crying*] My God, my God, Carl,

and to look at him it seem he's smiling…

Trumpets sound, loud banging on the outside door. It opens wide and we see a luxurious carriage—which we recognize, notwithstanding the gaudy decorations, as the one in which Stadelmann traveled—and four knights in full uniform on white horses richly saddled and plumed. In front of all of them the Messenger, with a sealed envelope in his hand. The whole group is unreal, phantasmagoric and operatic.

MESSENGER: In the name of the free city of Frankfurt I must deliver this envelope, sealed by the burgomaster, to Mr. Carl Wilhelm Stadelmann, asking the same to return a standard signed receipt.

AN OLD MAN: He cannot…

MESSENGER: Certainly he can, everyone can, if he does not do so it is because he doesn't wish to and if he has gotten into trouble, he could have been more careful, the Office cannot think of everything.

Here [*opens the envelope*] is the resolution with which the city of Frankfurt extends to the worthy Mr. Stadelmann a life-long pension, assigning to him in addition a house with garden, the maintenance of which will be provided by the same city of Frankfurt. I invite therefore Mr. Stadelmann to come forward, to sign and follow me to his new residence.

[*Trumpet blasts. We hear a voice that sounds like Goethe's:* "Stadelmann, sign the receipt!"]

STEFFI: He is not here...

MESSENGER: What do you mean, he is not here? The Office has him here. There is little time, the road is long and we have other places to visit, we cannot wait, it is already the third time today that we have arrived too late, to be truthful, from when I have had this duty, we have always arrived too late, and so the envelopes pile up and the houses with garden remain empty. I am sorry but without a standard signed receipt...

[*Trumpet blasts; messenger, carriage and knights disappear, the door shuts*]

THE DOCTOR: [*drawing near the Director, after a few moments' pause*] Well then, as usual, we can notify the university...

DIRECTOR: No, this time not, tell the institute that for their anatomy lessons they can look for a cadaver somewhere else, it's not that they are lacking... it is the stated desire of Her Highest Serene Grand Duchess. Understand, it is in respect to Goethe's memory...

[*Curtain*]

Claudio Magris

VOICES

Voices

276504, yes, that's right. Maybe 326429 is better. Why maybe, certainly there is no comparison, with that sweet and ironic inflection, deep as snow. But a warm, soft snow, a supple blanket to pull over your head, as sled dogs do, liking it under there, in the warmth... But one thing at a time. Even with voices you must respect the timing and situation. Especially with voices, otherwise, if someone opens her mouth at the wrong moment, even the most beautiful, it's a disaster, like trying to tune a cello in a bar, while at the next table they're playing an accordion and singing bawdy songs... But this is 276504's moment. There, three rings, then the music...

"I'm happy again singing and dancing in the rain. I'm dancing and singing in the rain... This is 276504. Sorry but I'm not at home. If you like you can leave a message after the beep. Thanks and bye."

Who knows why bye... yesterday she was still saying, "I'll call you when I return"... And now, instead, bye. That shameless informality, I wouldn't like it even if it were meant only for me. If I think that whoever, even just by mistake...Imperious, confrontational.

She must have raised her throat slightly, that white, fleshy throat, ready to maul. What am I saying, with that voice it is she who grabs you like a bear, a white bear, but not me, thanks, I am not getting caught. I know all to well how it will end up, but before she puts out her paw with those beautiful claws, bap, I've already put down the receiver and the cage stays empty. After the beep, on the other end, she'll hear nothing.

But who knows why, after all, she redid the recording, what must have come over her, like that, all of a sudden, to change the words, take out a verb and stick in a bye...And when? Between six in the afternoon yesterday and now, so probably late last night, going to bed, taking off her clothes, a perfumed voice, a naked woman's voice...Bye—not bad, after all, spoken from under the blankets. I deserve it, after this much time, that formal you of insurance policies was unjust, so anonymous and uncaring.

I have to hurry, it's the right moment for 572441, I'm still barely in time, if I don't take too long and it turns out that she's already back and she answers herself, like that other time—What a disaster. She should have just gotten in, without any time to disconnect the answering machine, so that when the phone rang her voice began to answer, but a few seconds later she jumped right in, while I was still listening to that intonation, a little somber, dark, severe...How distasteful and embarrassing, when that fluid, controlled calm was interrupted and she picked up intrusive, hurried, rude..."Who's this?" It wasn't even a real voice, just a clipped mumbling, like someone puffing or panting or yelling when you step on her foot. In no way was that talking.

A real, understanding, necessary voice is only the recorded one, just as a real word is only the one we write on paper, calm, alone in our own room—out there, beyond the window, the sky is empty, it whitens like an ever more pale face, the sun has disappeared and the blood has all drained away, there isn't any more....Above, in the narrow courtyard between the houses, the sky is a marble face. Even the paper is white and the words are there, black and blue, in fine calligraphy, the true, silent, orderly words, not those we blather in the push and pull of people and things. So it is with the pure recorded voice on the answering machine: phrased like music, free.

What long, immense afternoons, listening to real voices, careful not to let myself become bewildered in that enchantment, forgetting to watch the clock and letting myself get surprised by those false ones—luckily I discovered them in time, the voices. It was when I met Laura, well, more or less met, I saw her in the office, on the third floor, fire and theft claims, as she was going to punch her time card. Tall, almost clumsy in her slightly unbalanced walk, her head a little inclined towards her shoulder, black black hair and eyes looking intense and anxious, passionate. There was a tremor in those eyes, but also a great deal of courage, the relentless courage of a child alone in the night... I followed, I saw the time card with her first and last name. Laura is a tender and dark name, shadow of boughs and leaves, of an arm that presses your head and eyes against her breast...

So I traced her in the phone book and called her. The answering machine picked up; a self-absorbed, irrevocable voice; a court in which you feel judged and are glad. I, after the beep, said nothing, you understand. I am not ready to speak truly. Sure, in the office or out on the street, I shout, grumble, whisper, yell, I even clear my throat and cough, but this is not speaking.

I hung up, as was proper. The next day, I saw her in the office café, that's on the second floor, near the headquarters of the term life division. It was touch and go, what incredible luck. Another minute and who knows what might have happened, I would have been ruined—as I was approaching, hesitant, looking for something to say to her, she turned toward the counter and said, "A coke." As I watched her stunned, terrified by that strident, tense tone, she added, taking the can in her hand, "OK." Crude, mouth wide open in a broad and vulgar pronunciation, those vowels indecent as the breath of someone who doesn't use a toothbrush or toothpaste.

She was still there, with her Coca-Cola, in the eternity of her squalor, and I, almost like a rebound, was already at the phone in the corner of the bar, the coin already dropped in the machine like the blast of a counterattack. The drawbridge lowers and the knight enters the field to accept the challenge, and I had dialed her number. At the other end was Laura, Laura's true voice, enchanting and flowing like a wave, saying she wasn't home and inviting you to leave a message. Meanwhile I saw her in front of me, a few yards away, I heard the words she was saying to a colleague, the forced tone, a little higher than proper, bogus. I felt sorry for the young man who was trying to be witty with her, because he had only the simulacrum and I the real Laura, her voice, her immortal soul, safe from the miseries of hoarseness, of a cold, shortness of breath, fatigue.

It's the voices that count. Indeed, they are the only ones that exist. Bodies seem to make a lot of noise and occupy a lot of space, but they are just shadows, that disappear when the sun goes down. You just have to watch them leaving the office. All those employees crowding out the big front doors look like who knows what, a throng that's blocking everything, but barely outside they disperse like scraps of paper swept away by the wind, they disappear around the corner and the streets are suddenly once again deserted.

Bodies vanish, those of women don't actually exist. If you squeeze them you are left with air in your hands, like wanting to hug the tits of those film stars on the posters. Big and hard as melons, but they slip through your fingers, just a little rain and those posters drip and tear, legs and breasts and bottoms torn to pieces by the wind that scatters them and what we saw we saw, it's all a con. Every time I put my hands on a woman I didn't touch anything, except for a greedy roundness, only the flat and smooth surface of a publicity poster. The bodies aren't there, it's a trick like at an amusement park or the movies, when you put on the 3-D glasses and you think you see a mountain of things, but if you take off the glasses you realize that it's all an act. I took them right off, I'm the only one who goes around without them. Luckily all those others, who wear them on their noses, cannot tell.

The voices are everywhere, real, corporal; they arrive from all directions, they attack, they hide, they pretend to retreat and suddenly they jump out again, they resound in your head, just turn the corner and it's all a shouting, screeching, whispering. The other day I threw a piece of paper into the garbage container, I'm a civic-minded person. As I lifted the cover, even in there it was all a guffawing, grunting, rustling, giggling. I shut the cover and left calmly, I'm not the kind to get easily frightened. By now I know the world, it would be like fearing traffic because of all those cars cutting in and out from every corner, though, let's admit it, in the thick of it, it kind of gets to you.

But we shouldn't let ourselves be fooled, those are not the real voices, it's impossible for people to speak this way. Laura, for instance, doesn't actually speak the way we hear her talk at the bar. They want to make us believe it, to make us disgusted with women and then with all the rest. To take real life away from us and make us live in this filthy mess, but we don't have to fall for it. If we give in, if we let them take away our taste for women, for voices and for the world in general, we become servants and the accomplices to servitude. The world is real, vast and rich, full of real voices, of women.

I have had a lot of women—voices of real women, not those dolls you see and hear on the street. Very beautiful, different, harsh, tender, bold, timid. For God's sake, I'm not bragging. Don Giovanni's catalog is disgusting; every catalog is stupid, because every voice is unique and unrepeatable and is worth far more than the flatterer who waylaid them. Humility, this is what the voices teach us.

In fact, if there is a virtue I'm glad about, it is humility, patience. One needs method. Above all—the easiest isn't worth talking about—you need to get hold of the phone number. Without directly asking for it, that's obvious. Then you need to figure out the right times, to be sure of phoning when they aren't at home. Checking their hours, habits, comings and going, pauses for meals, the inner-workings of their days off and holidays. It's extremely distasteful calling a voice and hearing oneself answered by a crude and careless person. It's like going into the toilet and seeing your beloved sitting on the can, it is not a nice thing.

It's not enough to know her hours. If she lives with someone, you have to take care to call at those times when the other isn't there to answer, or else you have to hang up and that is vulgar. If it's the husband or lover, he will get jealous, banal as that may be, and it's not right to bother anyone. I am not jealous. I'm not interested in who lives with them, just as I'm not interested in who stands around them on the subway. Anyway they never listen to them as I do; they are excluded from their intimacy. If one of those poor housemates answers, I would be ashamed to keep quiet while he asks who it is. I would feel like some maniac who molests people.

Keeping quiet while her voice speaks, the voice of one of them, that's different; even when the recording is over I stay and listen to the silence that follows. What can I say, even if I felt like it? When the sun sinks behind those big gray barracks and for an instant the windows light up here and there like candles on a Christmas tree, or when you listen to Schubert lieder, you don't start in talking, but bow your head and keep quiet.

Worst of all—and it's because of this that you have to be absolutely sure they are not at home—is if she has come back and forgotten to turn off the answering machine, as in fact happened the other day. The real her starts answering, and you are blessedly listening, careful not to loose the least nuance, and then all at once, bang, someone, the other, intervenes and you hear an aggressive and annoyed "Who's this?" It has happened to me twice and with 283770 in particular it was a real shock, like a yawn while making love. That's a far off, absent voice, that comes from beyond the sea. I passed the most beautiful hours of my life listening and one day that melody, familiar and always new, was interrupted. She must have come back home for some unexpected reason, she so regular and habitual, and she intervened so crudely with a disgraceful "Helloo?" I didn't call her anymore; when something's over, it's over.

I don't call just once, why be so tough on yourself and deny yourself happiness? I call, I listen, I hang up, I call back. Every time there is something different, a imperceptible nuance that might be lost on anyone, but not for a lover like me; a slightly prolonged delay, a sweetness a little more reserved, a word that resounds a little more deeply in the heart, a more decisive or capricious tone. Each time it's different. Let's hear 276504 again.

"I'm happy again singing and dancing in the

rain... I'm dancing and singing in the rain... This is 276504. Sorry but I'm not at home. If you like you can leave a message after the beep. Thanks and bye."

There, this time there is a small lie. Of all the phrases, now only the bye rings true. I'm hearing her say it with that saucy air, half in bed, with one of her long legs playing with the blankets. We understand right away that she's not sorry at all, as instead just a while ago, but who cares. It's useless to tell me that it is always the same recording, I know it too, but... there, it's like looking at a photograph. It's always the same, but each time something new emerges and disappears. Now there is a melancholy in that fold of the mouth that was laughing before—and is still laughing, we understand, the photograph is still the same, but as you look at it again you see a painful wrinkle in that smile, a more sharply cut line, a deeper shadow.

It's there, in that figure, something changing while you watch. Once, at the office, they gave me a test: it was interesting and the psychologist was a little nosey if likable. Anyway, better than the other, so condescending, with his white, nauseating caramels. That psychologist showed me a drawing and told me to stare at it a while. First I saw a black cup on a white background and then, suddenly, two faces, two profiles that looked at each other grinning. There, in that figure, something clicked, something changed, it was like a flash of lightening, a landscape. The psychologist told me that it was exactly because of this that they were called bi-stable figures. Even if you look at the daytime winter sky, a light in the west gripping your heart and the black black trees against that light, you look and all is still and equal, the sky empty and clear, an inextinguishable light that will never pass because it is a color that lights up inside the air—and all at once, in an instant, it's dark. Something has changed in the sky, in the trees and the branches; they are always and still there, but they are not the same.

Then it's a voice, a woman's voice...it's like that hollow, diaphanous sky, never ending with corpses inside, plunging down without hitting bottom. Every day I call 326429, three times a day, except for Sundays and other holidays: in the morning after 8:30, just after she has left, around eleven and in the middle of the afternoon. Each time I feel as if I've reached the depths of that voice, the soft riverbed in which the words vanish in a murmur, sigh of nighttime waters, sweet darkness of ancient sea—For a second, but only the flicker of an instant, I seem to recall a remote time, when I was a fish and I had never seen the shore and there had yet to be thousands of millennia before fisherman would exist. Or when I was almost not a fish and I swam in the sweetest and darkest waters, and I hear a woman's voice which was that sea in which I swam and that voice was the same thing as that water and it was everything.

But I never touch bottom; the next time I fall even deeper, 326429 has many layers. Clear, gloomy, brazen, that teases you only to slam the door in your face. Sometimes you need to slap it around, as often ends up being the case with women. Then you realize that there is also tenderness, the grand pity of a real woman for a man, who is always a child. It's only there, when we listen on the phone to those voices, absolute and universal, recorded or rather aimed at everybody, beyond every little private concern, that we finally come to understand the true nature of woman—Mary with the child at her breast. Otherwise those marionettes that we see all over, coquettes or crybabies, prick-teasers or ball-breakers, they leave my heart in my shoe.

Even 722816 is different every time. Shameless, submissive, remorseful, indulgent. I know her better than she knows herself, because she doesn't hear herself on the phone. She recorded that message but doesn't know all that there is in it, melancholy, worries, arrogance, vanity... She's also crazy about constantly changing her recorded message, who knows why. To tell the truth these external changes don't interest me very much. They are irrelevant in respect to those unconscious, dizzy changes hidden in the repetition of the same message, those pauses that all of a sudden become more profound, like dark fissures in the ground, ditches in which we stick our foot and tumble, down down down, to the bottom of that voice's darkness, into the throat's cavity, into the dark cave... Or that shivers, that vibrates every once in a while in a word, in silence, and everything around it stops, the world is immobile and hanging, enormous, empty...

Anyway, I have to dedicate my full attention even to those banal changes. Yesterday, for instance, she said: "I am not at home, leave a message or, if it's something urgent, call me at 352786." Hasty, as if talking right to you, with the insignificance of an off-hand conversation. This morning, instead, slow, deliberate, pouting lips, kissable mouth. "This is 722816. Call back later or let us know who you are." I listened to it three times in a row, this despotic and impudent invitation. Sometimes, the music comes first, sometimes after or other times no music at all. Why all these changes, all this recording, erasing, choosing a text, rerecording? Maybe she decides to address a different interlocutor, unknown but different, who demands another tone? But how dare to make me suffer like this, when it's someone else, a maniac, who might be calling her. Our relationship goes back years, and some Johnny come lately has no place interfering. It's not right. I won't allow them to take her away.

Everybody takes everything from me, the butcher knife tears away the flesh piece by piece and the mothers there shopping for their children, standing in line waiting their turn in that smell of blood, how can you think of Christmas dinner among those dangling chunks of meat? For me it's the same, they keep answering the phone less and less and each time a piece of me falls and disappears into that void. That they may even let themselves be accosted in the streets, this vulgarity is not my concern, but that they don't allow themselves to be called when they are not at home.

I know how to get even, how to pay them back in kind. I am not lacking women. If one of them betrays me, I don't waste any time calling another. I even have a table with all the exact times. 482781 can only be called in the afternoons, because she starts working at 2p.m. 253612 is more complicated, an alternating schedule, Monday, Tuesday, Wednesday mornings and the other days in the afternoons, even Saturdays, when she goes shopping. But it's risky. Once she was home and I had to hang up right away. I deserved it, because you never should feel so secure, or especially mind that you don't become set in your ways and automatically assume that she too feels like it at the same time you do. Love means respect, not taking anything for granted, adapting oneself delicately to the state of mind of the beloved.

I am sick and tired of 391529, she is a careless creature, without regular hours. You never know what to expect, and I can't be bothered so I've cut her loose. Also because, except for 276504, 572441, 326429, and 722816, who live alone, in other cases I have to keep track of the husband's or the partner's hours. Then with 695723, there's even her mother, an old bag that yells into the receiver every time. It's not right that it always has to be me who has to regulate myself according to others. I too have the right to my say and to call whenever I feel like it, one can't after all switch desire on and off.

Sometimes it bugs me to have to call 482781 in the middle of the afternoon: it's a time I don't like, it's bad for digestion. My food sits on my stomach and repeats, I feel the bile in my mouth and in my heart and it's not the right time for courtship—I want to sit in front of a window and watch the hanging laundry flapping in the wind, for hours, while the courtyard wall slowly changes color.

Even the one at 276504 is more than a little demanding. She is always dictating the hour at which she wants to be called; for me it's a disastrous time, but how can you disobey, once you have heard that "Bye" you're lost. So I call her even if I don't feel like it. Other times I get unstoppable urge to call her, call all of them. It happens in the morning, after hours and hours of insomnia. It's atrocious not to sleep, the windows whiten like foam floating on black waters—if I only could call at that moment, but they are still in bed, warm and heavy. Under the blankets there is the smell of stables, and then the answering machines are not switched on, so you would only hear the voices swollen with sleep, grunting of sows, and everything would be all over. So I have to toss and turn and wait until its time for work, school, shopping, and meanwhile the desire might be gone. Before I was all taut and burning and then picked up the phone just like this, out of habit, because I'm faithful, but if nobody answered it would be even better for me.

Besides, even later at the office, I am the one who

has to answer the phone, pass news along, give out information, take messages, picking up a receiver with my left hand while I'm holding in my right the one into which I am already speaking, then another phone rings and I wedge it between my ear and shoulder. More rings, it's horrible, voices booming from every side, each one thinking he's the one and only and acting as if I'm there just for him, arrogant, greedy, shrill, dull voices, something's about to bust inside me…

Even if my voices, the real ones, would call me all at the same time it would be horrible, as in a harem all those women all over you and you haven't yet begun that you already have to stop because of another phone ringing. Only a eunuch can be comfortable in a harem. At night, when I toss in bed, I hear all that ringing, spears sticking into my brain, the dentist's drill, and I get up and swallow a couple of pills but it's useless, everything keeps ringing.

This is why I only call their answering machines: how could I call them in person, treat them as the world treats me? I respect women, respect them all, even the ones I don't like. I would never allow myself to enter their heads, the ring is a rape, ripping and spreading, it's horrible. I would give rapists the death penalty and don't try to come and tell me they couldn't help themselves. I don't buy it, desire gets flaccid so quick, and then if it's that bad they can go to the toilet and calm down all by themselves. It's disgusting, but always better than to do violence to others and phone when they don't expect it, surprising and jumping on top of them.

The other night, while I was tossing in bed plugging my ears up with a pillow and everything around me was ringing and screaming, I realized that something monstrous must have happened and we were not aware of it. It wasn't a dream, no, if I were only dreaming. At least it would have meant that I had slept and even a nightmare, given the closed eyelids, is better than being awake and looking around with eyes wide open. I realized that the world is an enormous telephone exchange and it's from there that everything is run. God has gone away and somebody has taken his place, the lord of darkness and clatter—evil is noisy, an uproar, in fact saints pray in silence, don't bother anyone, don't phone anyone. From over there someone calls without stopping, calls to assault, order, torment, to block our breathing, smelling, touching, tasting, loving.

Although I did not let myself panic, I defended myself. I cut the phone cords, first at home then at the office. Anyway, to call my voices all I have to do is go down to the cafe across the street. But I waited to long and it was already late. Somebody, the last time I was asleep, I don't remember when, must have opened my head and tied some telephone wires directly to my brain. In fact the scar is still there, right here, under my hair. Even at the office the next day, the wires were once again connected, everything was working and ringing all over again.

I like to call, not be called. I am respectful, I've already said that, but I am a man and I won't completely give up the initiative. I know how to take my time, wait for the right moment, that's part of the experience; who understands that doesn't jump in like a boy, but anyway, I want to be the one to call. It would be so beautiful if nobody called, ever, a silent, peaceful world... And I, just me, dialing the numbers... But even there, in that other place, something is beginning to happen, the traps are everywhere. Just a while ago I dialed 281531, always so caressing and velvety... I called her at 9a.m., the right hour, and in fact she wasn't there. But it wasn't her voice that answered. It was another thing, metallic, asexual, neutral: "THIS-IS-28–15–31-PLEASE-CALL-BACK-AF-TER-TWO-IN-THE-AF-TER-NOON..."

I knew that it's called an *answering service*—you

don't tape, you don't record your voice, you punch keys, numbers and out comes this…No, it's not a voice but it speaks—an iron throat, a breath that you put together and take apart like pieces of a mechanism, a doll freezing cold as the railing in the park in winter, that to the touch, even just to look at it, brings chills. Even the glass in my always shut windows are this cold, I don't know how they got there, who installed them. Once, of course, they weren't there, it was summer, it was always summer, the windows were open and I could lean out from the sill.

It's just another trick of his over there, the guy from the phone exchange, total envy for the beautiful things I have had. He does everything to destroy me, tricks, ambushes…God knows how many ambushes, wounds, with how much effort I saved myself each time. As in that ditch—I was sinking and losing ground, I was already lost, I couldn't find my way anymore. In that downpour, the streets between houses, high above the roofs, there was spring flooding, rivers brim full that were knocking down and sweeping everything away. They had carried me off, but I made it, I played dead and when the waters receded I was still there, holding tight. I opened my eyes again and I even winked at that clear sky, drained of water, at that stupid sun, sitting there like a ball left high and dry at low tide.

And many, many other cowardly moves. They even took away the streetcar stop in front of my house, so I have to go to the office on foot. In winter it gets cold, the snow wets your socks and shoes and then freezes. Buses stop where they feel like it, every day the stops change, so it's useless the try to figure out the schedule. It's better to analyze it carefully, to figure out where they can switch them, to guess at their logic and be standing at that place when they think they had left you behind at some just cancelled stop.

Once there was a whole squad of those crooks, who were pretending to open the manhole covers and they made me take a longer route, telling me I couldn't go through there. I was ready to punch them in the nose, and then I realized this is exactly what they wanted and I wouldn't fall for it. I laughed, made a bow and called them boss to stay on their good side. They laughed, they believed I didn't understand a thing, and when they realized I'd pulled it off, it was too late; I was already out of range. I took a roundabout, very roundabout route, the office was always further off, the center of a huge circle, a huge circle of snow. They were waiting for me, there in the middle, already set to pounce, but I kept moving in an ever wider path, in enormous circles—I surrounded them, circled them, I had them in the palm of my hand.

Anyway, they couldn't run me down. I had the voices and they helped me, they kept me together. Anyone who has never tried it cannot know how love helps in facing trouble. A woman who stays at your side, when you are upset she talks to you in just the right way, with that easy smile they have, it means everything. In this way they have realized that as long as those women were with me, I wasn't afraid of anything and they couldn't touch me at all. Now they are taking them away, one after the other. Instead there is only that inhuman non-voice, that steel thing that talks, and mockingly they have given it a nice slick name, answering service, a real come on. I don't want that out-of-tune, strident metal. I want the voices, the women, down to those flesh and blood vulgar ones. Though it's late, too late to call them, even the bye of 276504 has disappeared, replaced by that metallic scraping. I knew that love sooner or later had to be over, everything comes to an end and I don't pretend anything is forever. But it was over too fast, and all of a sudden. A poor devil ought to have the right to make a phone call every once in a while.

So I have decided to sabotage those gadgets—I refuse to call them by that slick, high-sounding name—and I began with 276504. I knew when nobody would be home and I tried to get in to destroy the device, the wicked spell. I would have freed the captive princess and recovered her voice. But they saw me while I was climbing over the balcony. The super must have been in on it and called them. They already were spread out everywhere; I should have expected a trap. They jumped on me, but I took a rock and whacking them left and right, I broke through and escaped to this barn in the woods. I hurt myself a little but it doesn't matter, it's just a little blood, mine I think... The woods are deep and they won't find me. Let them think that they have me, all the better. At night I will go to one of those telephone booths along the road and I will try dialing other numbers. Maybe there is still a real voice out there. What counts is not giving in....

GREEN INTEGER
Pataphysics and Pedantry

Douglas Messerli, *Publisher*

Essays, Manifestos, Statements, Speeches,
Maxims, Epistles, Diaristic Notes, Narrative,
Natural Histories, Poems, Plays, Performances,
Ramblings, Revelations and all such ephemera
as may appear necessary to bring society into a
slight tremolo of confusion and fright at least.

❧

Individuals may order Green Integer titles
through PayPal (*www.paypal.com*). Please pay
the price listed below plus $2.00 for postage to
Green Integer through the PayPal system.
You can also visit our site at *www.greeninteger.com*
If you have questions please feel free to e-mail
the publisher at *info@greeninteger.com*
Bookstores and libraries should order
through our distributors:
USA and Canada: Consortium Book
Sales and Distribution
United Kingdom and Europe:
Turnaround Publisher Services
Unit 3, Olympia Trading Estate,
Coburg Road, Wood Green,
London N22 6TZ UK

Works of Theater and Film

Eleanor Antin [Yevegeny Antiov] *The Man Without a World: A Screenplay* [1-892295-81-4] $10.95

Djuna Barnes *The Antiphon* [1-899295-56-3] $12.95

Charles Bernstein *Shadowtime* [1-933382-00-7] $11.95

Lee Breuer *La Divina Caricatura* [1-931243-39-5] $14.95

Luis Buñuel *The Exterminating Angel* [1-931243-36-0] $11.95

Louis-Ferdinand Céline *Ballets without Music, without Dancers, without Anything* [1-892295-06-8] $10.95

—— *The Church: A Comedy in Five Acts* [1-892295-78-4] $13.95

Anton Chekhov *A Tragic Man Despite Himself: The Complete Short Plays* [1-931243-17-4] $24.95

Carlos Felipe [with Julio Matas and Virgilio Piñera] *Three Masterpieces of Cuban Drama* [1-892295-66-0] $12.95

Maria Irene Fornes *Abingdon Square* [1-892295-64-4] $9.95

Armand Gatti *Two Plays: The 7 Possibilities for Train 713 Departing from Auschwitz* and *Public Song Before Two Electric Chairs* [1-9312433-28-x] $14.95

Elana Greenfield *Damascus Gate: Short Hallucinations* [1-931243-49-2] $10.95

Len Jenkin *Careless Love* [Sun & Moon Press: 1-55713-168-6] $9.95

James Joyce *On Ibsen* [1-55713-372-7] $8.95